AF587993

Dogs
in early New Zealand photographs

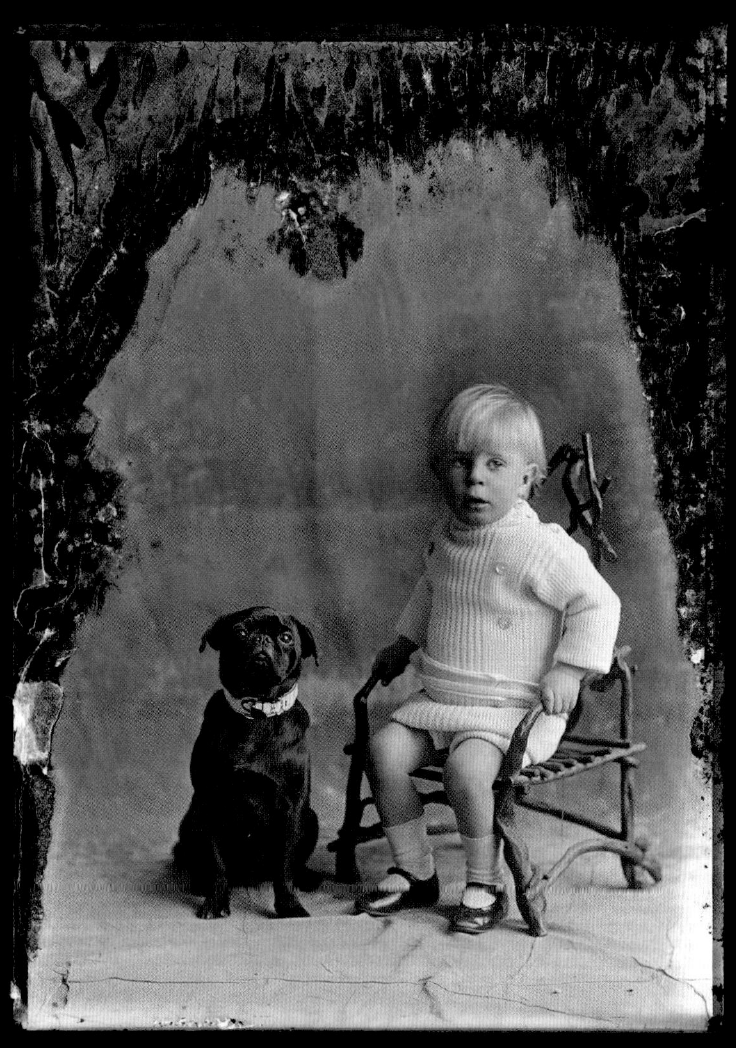

Dogs
in early New Zealand photographs

Introduction
by Mike White

Dogs in the frame

It was sitting in a glass cabinet, alongside several pieces of cast-off jewellery, near the till at the old Dunedin Hospice shop. My sister spotted it and thought it was just perfect: a small black-and-white photograph of a man and a dog. It had obviously been removed from someone's photograph album; black backing paper was still stuck to the photo. In the frame, the man leans back, thumbs tucked into braces, woollen trousers and jacket, his look a mix of amusement and affection. To his left, sitting on what looks like the stump of a vast tree, is a dog. *His* dog, you'd like to think. Handsome and proud.

My sister couldn't bear to leave them there, so paid ten cents to free them from the cabinet, and sent the photo to me because she knew I'd appreciate it. I have it on my windowsill, where a glance guarantees small joy at what it represents. Photos can do that. Especially photos with dogs.

Who they were and how they ended up in a Dunedin op shop will likely always be a mystery. And I don't mind that. I don't really need to know the names or context. The fact

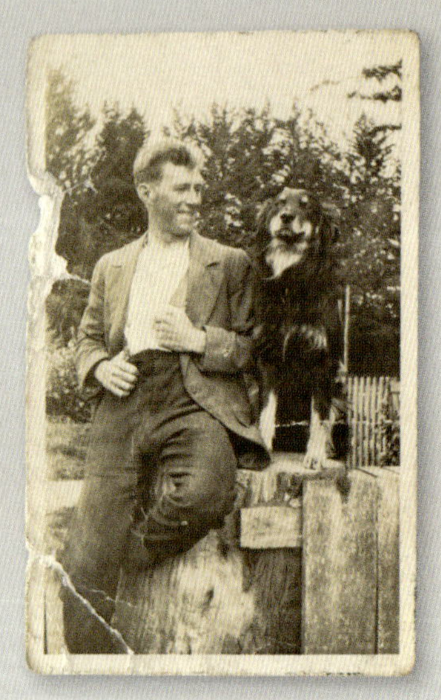

that for that split second they were so obviously happy in each other's company is charm enough.

The famous American photographer Elliott Erwitt once explained the attraction of his most celebrated subjects: 'I take a lot of pictures of dogs, because I like dogs, because they don't object to being photographed, and because they don't ask for prints.'

Erwitt's dog photos filled five books and countless metres on gallery walls, but most dog photos reach far more modest audiences. They generally dwell in family photo albums filed on high shelves, rarely opened, or they hide in electronic darkness on some forgotten hard drive, diluted by a thousand other photos of limited quality and consequence.

Nowadays, dog photos are snapped and shared via phones, instantly conveyed, fleetingly appreciated, then replaced by some subsequent mundanity that's seized the recipient's attention. But, as the wonderful and remarkable photos in this book demonstrate, there was a time when photographing dogs was much more deliberate, and the resultant prints lasted vastly longer than the half-life of an Instagram post.

From the mid-nineteenth century, a string of photographic studios operated throughout New Zealand, offering portraits with subjects seated against backdrops that ranged from rustic to exotic. Photographers employed bulky cameras with glass-plate negatives set atop heavy wooden stands, used only natural light and estimated exposure, given this was well before light meters. Exposures might have been seconds long – a nervous eternity when needing to avoid a blink or the slightest of movements. In the field, marginally more portable cameras and tripods were used, but approximating focus and exposure proved even more fraught.

The earliest photographs in this book were taken in the 1870s and the latest in the 1920s, about the time when ordinary people started to pick up cameras in large numbers. After 1920, when roll-film became widely available, and truly democratised photography, many studios went into decline, relinquishing their role as crucial centres for recording and documenting the well-dressed and well-to-do, the well-heeled, and, occasionally, their well-heeling companions.

The photos collected for this book notwithstanding, it would be wrong to think that dogs were commonplace in studio photos. Perhaps one in a hundred photos featured them. But when they did, they were incorporated in the same way they had been in artworks prior to the invention of photography in the early nineteenth century. One need only look at the sixteenth-century painting of Catherine of Aragon, Queen of England, clutching her pet monkey to understand the enduring urge to appear with animals.

Exactly why a few in these early New Zealand portraits chose to include dogs can only be surmised. For some it would have been a marker of wealth and status. For others, it perhaps hinted at empathy and a compassionate touch. But I'd guess that, for the majority, dogs were brought into photographs simply because they were part of the family, as loved and important as dogs have always been for so many.

Sometimes dogs were props, sometimes they were mascots, sometimes they were the stars of the photos reproduced here. But generally, they just shared the frame, and the note to history these photos have become. If you removed the dog from the photo, its attraction would shrink immeasurably. All you'd be left with are men in pressed suits and women in splendid hats, looking stiff and stilted, aware this is a special occasion but unsure quite how to respond.

Dogs aren't troubled by such things. They stay natural – the only state they know – and, in doing so, soften any photo they're in. Throughout the nearly two centuries we've been photographing dogs, human affectations and fashions have changed, but dogs have remained as they always have. They're pure like that, devoid of finery or artifice.

It's hard not to fall, and fall hard, for so many of these photos, where the dogs sit dutifully, ears lifted, tails stilled for a second. Fetching collies, *qui vive* terriers, willowy whippets, docile spaniels. Terror. Floss. Jack. Jumbo. Paddy. And an array of gorgeous unknowns . . . All dogs that people liked, who cared not a jot about the photographer intruding on their privacy, and who certainly didn't want prints.

The show-business adage to never work with children or animals is rooted in good sense. Taking photos of dogs is hard. I know, because I have tried it for decades, with far from frequent success. Blurred bodies, tips of noses sharp and the rest of them out of focus, alien green eyes from using a flash – I have made a hash of any number of dog photos. But some, a few, have worked.

My parents, wielding a Kodak Box Brownie, did the same thing, and our family's early photo albums feature plenty of dogs, many that pre-date me. Charlie. Tan. Lass. Some random puppies. If Dad is in them, he nurses a cigarette. Mum wears an apron.

Photos of dogs make chapters in our lives easier to remember, demarcate decades, are touchstones of past events and places. And they're fun to take. The slightly sad thing is, however, that dogs don't really understand photos. In the same way that they are perplexed or ambivalent when they spy themselves in a mirror, the concept of a photo is foreign in their world.

That sense of memory is less important for a dog than a potential opportunity, yesterday of less consequence than the possibility of now, or this afternoon, or tomorrow. Oh, memory is important, at the heart of their loyalty and love. But it isn't bounded by a rectangular frame, or stored in pixels. Crucially, the smell of what's in the image is absent. What's in front of a dog's nose is ultimately what guides it, and excites it, and photos rate poorly in this respect.

The fact the photos in this book have survived a century or more is due to a combination of serendipity and foresight. Many, like the images in this book, ended up in museum collections, to be stored and restored. But countless others vanished. Stories abound of entire studio inventories of negatives and prints simply being deemed valueless, and dumped. That a fraction remain is cause for celebration, and for gratitude to those who realised their importance, in time.

Some of the photos, of course, have true historical significance. The dogs Scott took to the Antarctic, including the heroic husky Osman (page 91). Paddy the Irish terrier, who went to war and survived Gallipoli (page 121). And the unstinting Betsey Jane, who accompanied explorer Charles Douglas on many of his adventures (page 51). Betsey Jane sadly disappeared on one epic trip, perhaps into a crevasse or over a flinty bluff. (She fared slightly better than another explorer's dog, Thomas Brunner's Rover. When Brunner's party ran desperately short of food while descending the Buller River in 1847, Rover was eaten in desperation, to stave off starvation.)

Others here are true working dogs, photographed alongside firefighters, sawmillers, miners and fishermen. They were dogs that knew nothing of the indulgences today's pets can enjoy, from orthopaedic beds and vitamin water to canine craniosacral therapy.

Most we know little about, not even their names or those of their owners. In the absence of these, there's temptation to imagine, and to invent stories to fill the gaps. I mean, who was 'NicK', whose name was emblazoned on a small suitcase with its taped-up handle, carried by a shaggy and shiny black spaniel (pages 84–85)? Even when it's sparse, the information accompanying some of the photos is priceless, though. I've found myself returning often to the photo of Cyril McCusker in uniform (pages 126–127), taken by his father after Cyril enlisted in the army at the beginning of the First World War. Beside him is a lovely huntaway/collie/retriever/somethingorother, its muzzle greying, its thick coat slicked on one flank, suggesting a recent swim, or a roll in something rural. It's taken near the Taylor Pass Road, just south of Blenheim. And given the age of the dog and Cyril – about twenty-three – you have to guess they've grown up together.

Years ago, I used to climb the same hills, all lichen-flecked rock and tussock, with my dog Gyp, a bitser who helped sustain me through my teenage years and early twenties. Just before I went overseas for a long stint, Gyp and I went up the Taylor Pass one last time, and as we climbed a hill I took photos of him, a happy dog in what was a happy place for us both. Like Cyril McCusker's father that day in 1914, I imagine, you took a photo because you didn't know what the future held and when you might see the subject again. You wanted that memory. Cyril survived the war. Gyp died before I got home.

My morning dog walk often takes me along the coast to a beach where dogs are allowed to wheel and bark and romp and swim without leash or petty legislation. They emerge from the water, sticks in mouths, fur flattened by the sea, and prance around with their trophies until they're ready to do it all again.

One morning, not that long ago, I arrived to find a woman standing alone. I scanned the beach but couldn't see an accompanying dog, which struck me as slightly strange on this stretch of sand and pīngao. As I came down the steps, she hurried towards me. 'Hello. Do you mind if I take a photo of your dog?' she asked, phone in hand, ready to go.

'No, fire away. But he might not stand still,' I warned, as Cooper circled, waiting for me to fetch a stick. I asked if she had a dog.

'Not anymore,' she said, with the slight silence afterwards that never needs to be filled. Dogs die, and the gap is vast. *Not anymore*. So now she took photos of other people's dogs while out walking. It gave her daily exercise some purpose, she said.

'The light is so lovely, this morning,' she enthused as Cooper returned triumphant from the shallows with a stick, and she tracked him up the beach. 'So proud!' she said.

I tried to get Cooper to stand still by holding the stick in front of him. He was having none of this, and danced up to snatch it. Eventually, after a couple more throws, he paused and posed, front paw cocked, ears up, eyes intent, and the woman got her photo. She showed it to me. He looked fantastic. She looked as pleased as Punch.

Cooper and I carried on, and left her with the beach to herself and another image to add to her collection. Who knows what she'll do with it, if she'll ever look at that photo of Cooper again, or send it out on social media for applause. It sort of doesn't matter. There was pleasure in the taking, in the mutual moment. That's enough. And who knows, decades down the line, just maybe, someone else might come across it, and briefly puzzle over it. A small frame to fill with their imagination and questions, just like so many of the photos in this book.

Unnamed dog. Unidentified beach. Unknown photographer. But something nearly all of us can instantly understand – and love.

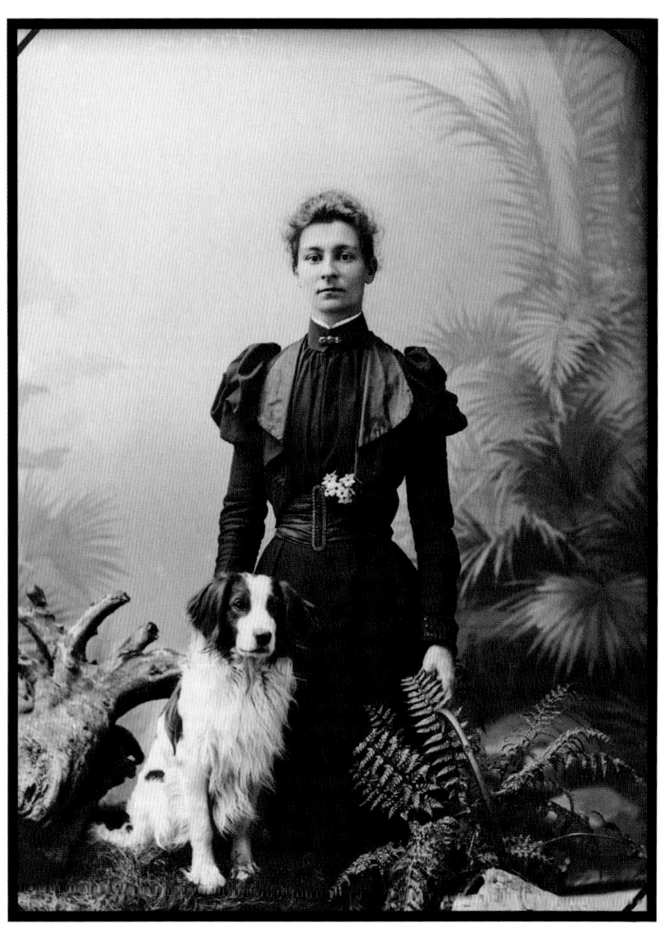

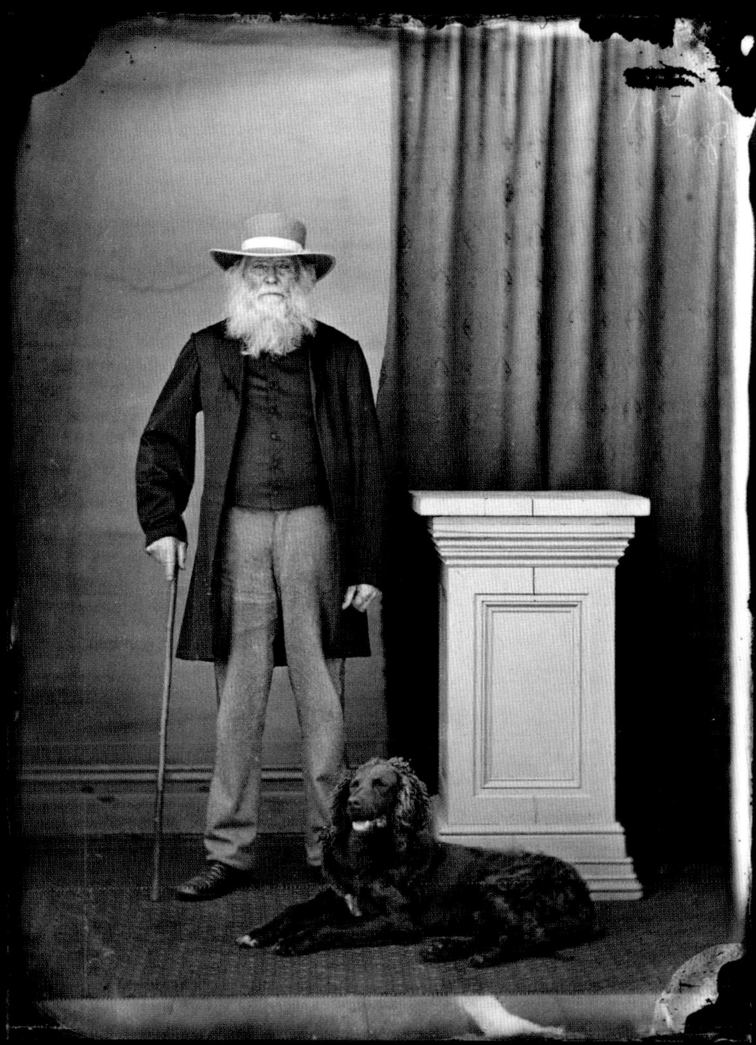

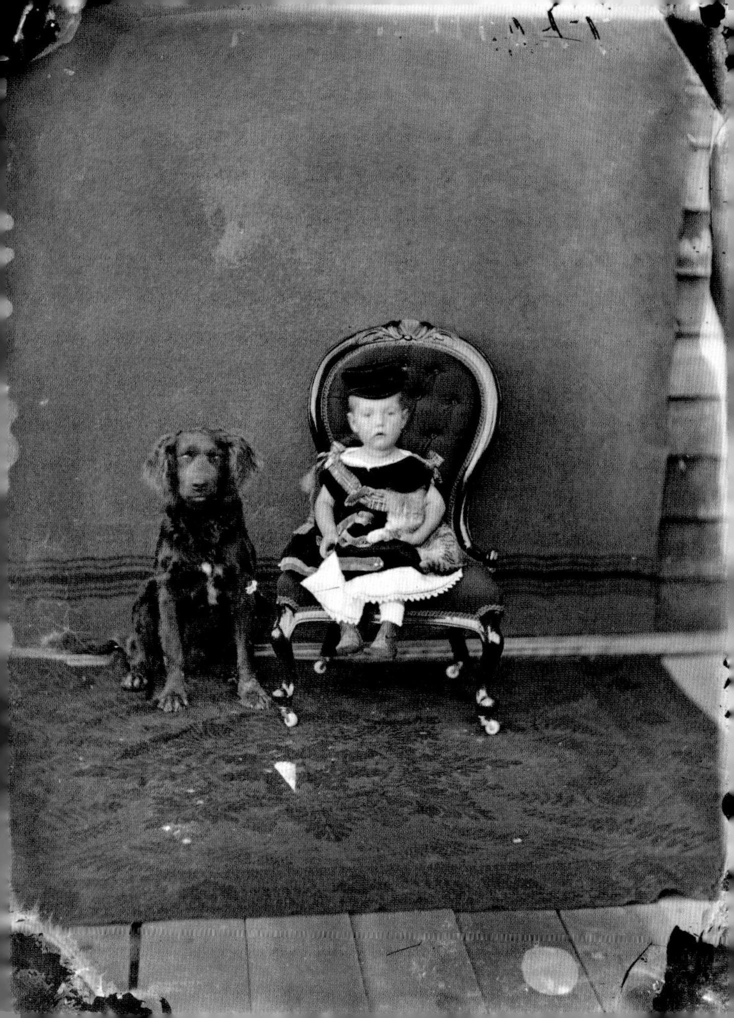

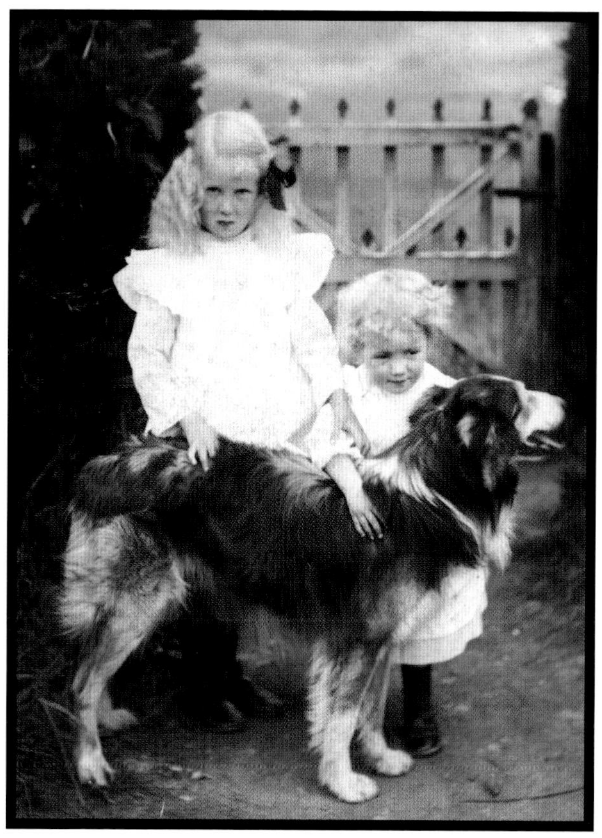

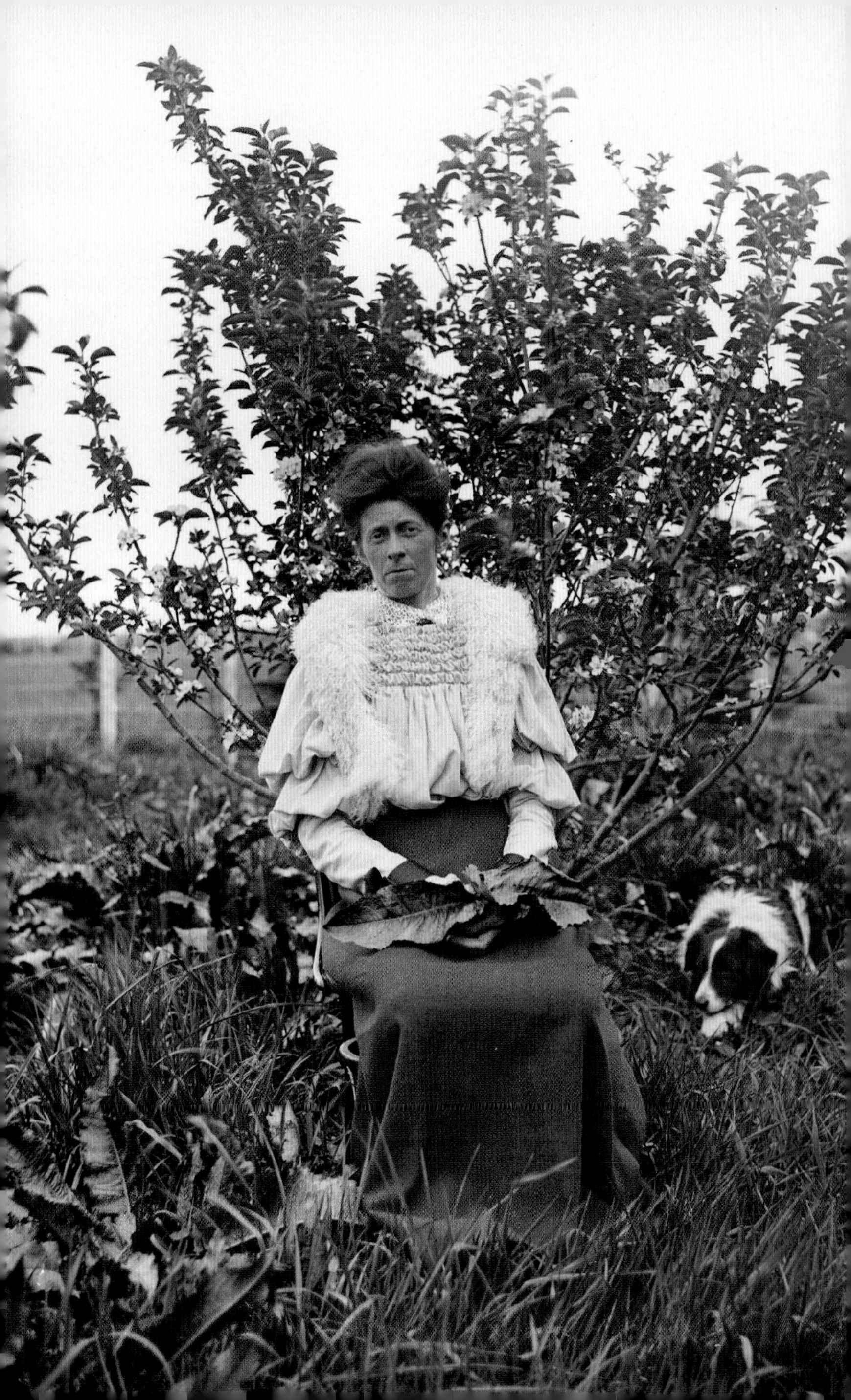

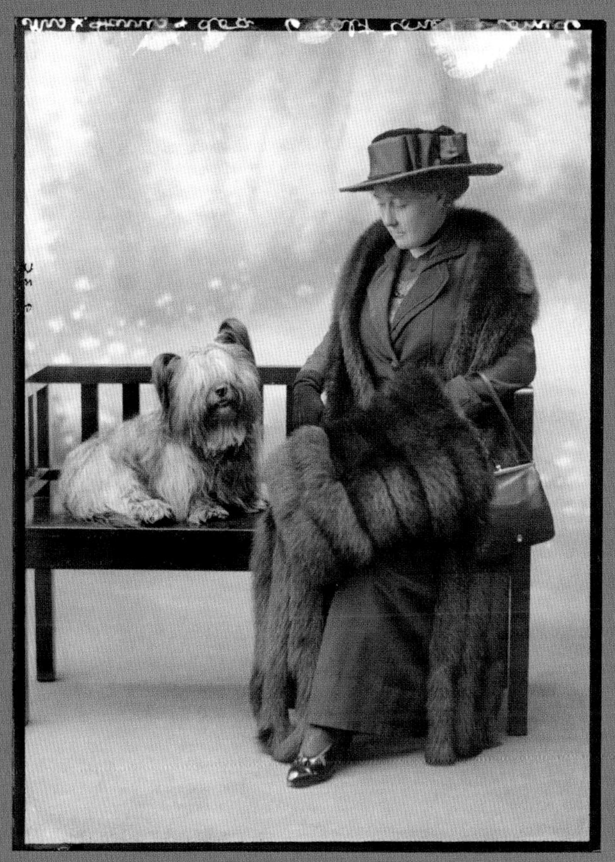

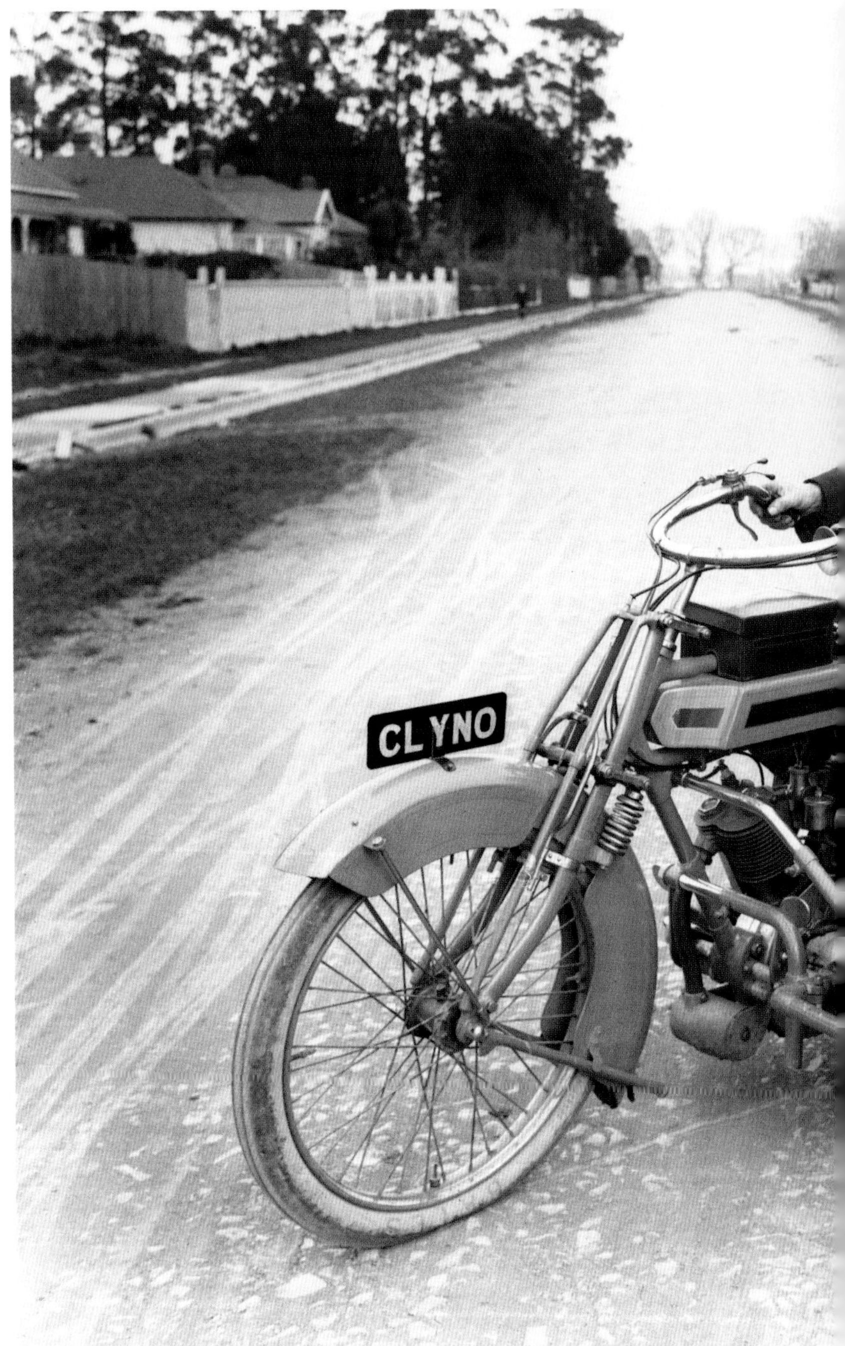
CLYNO

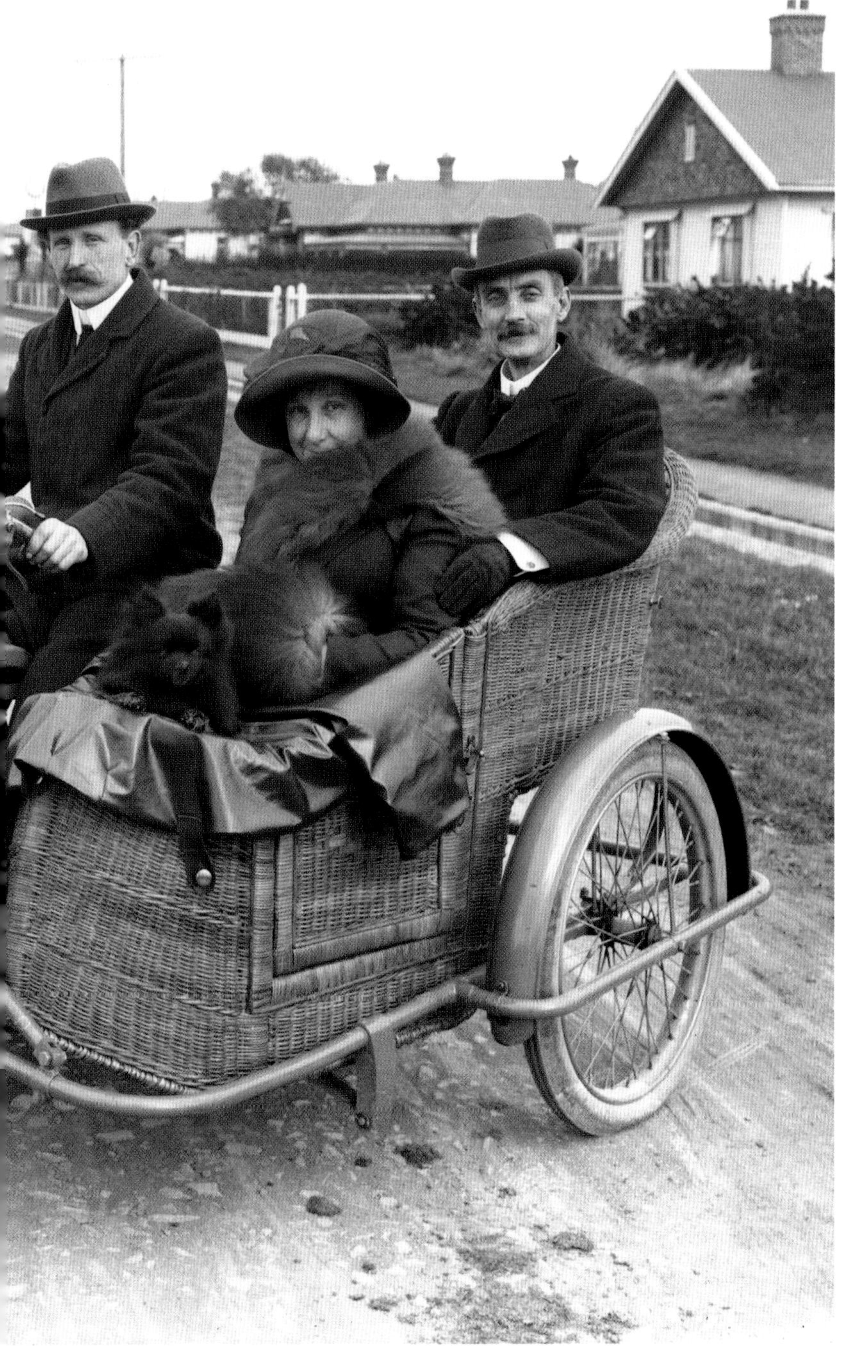

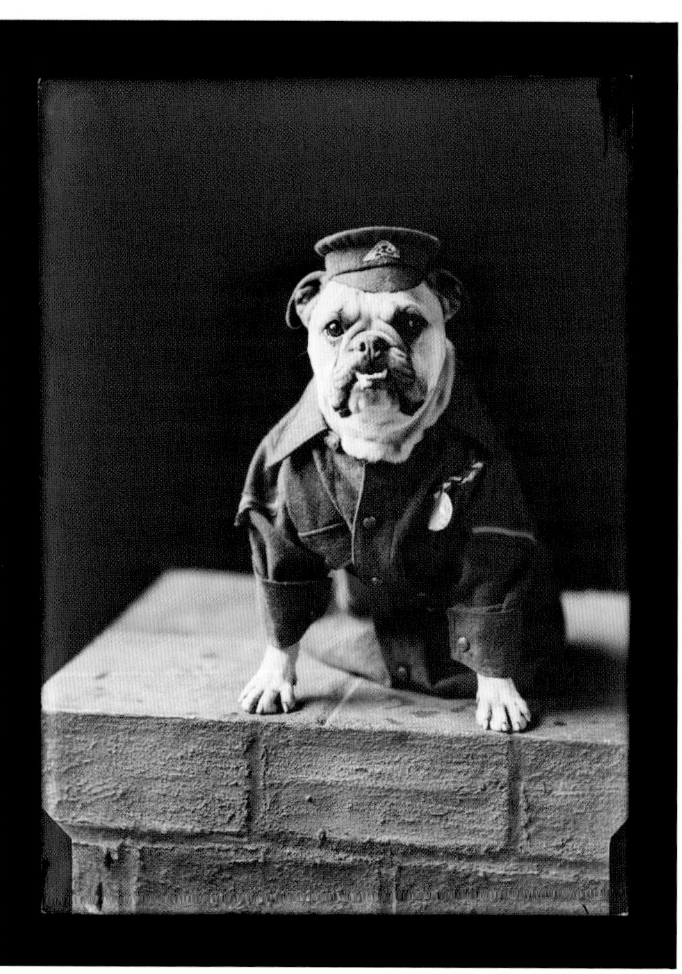

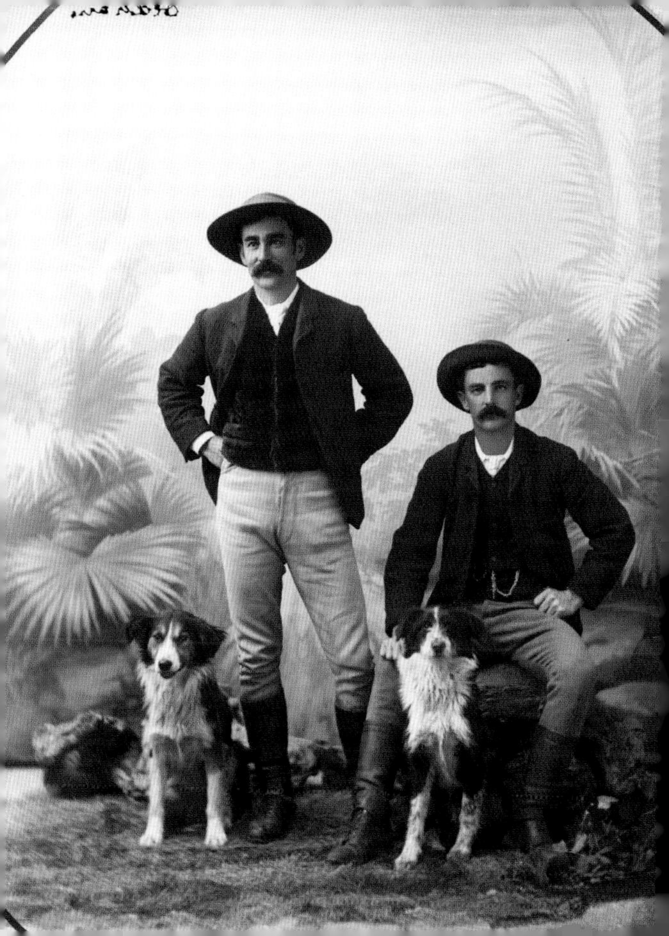

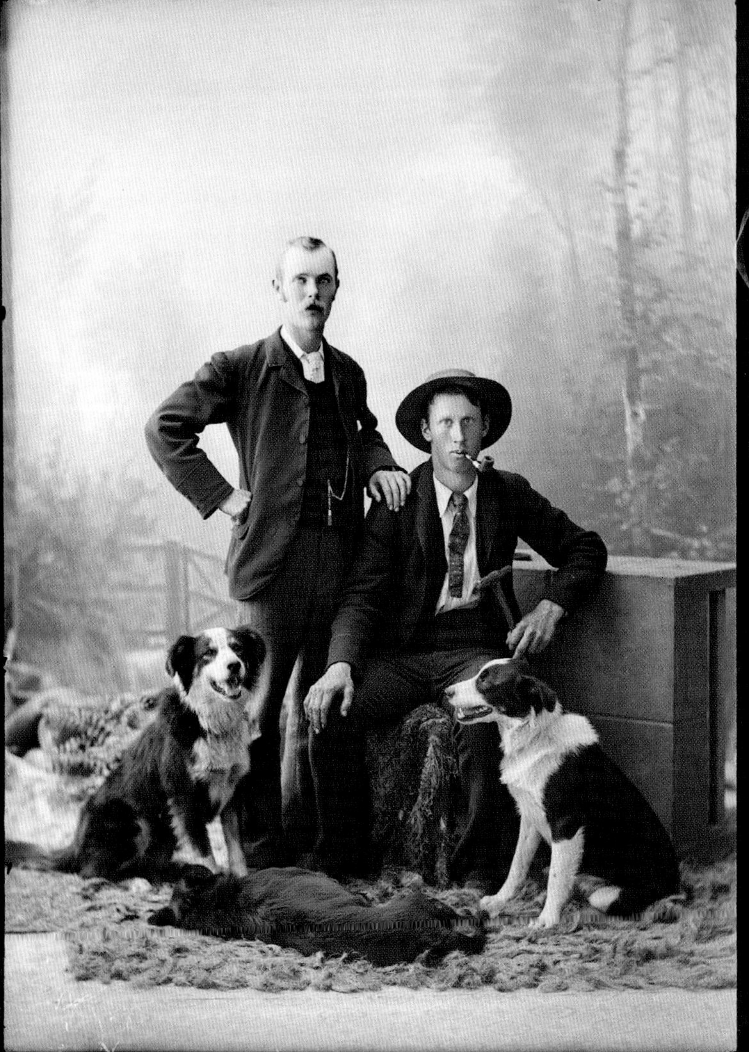

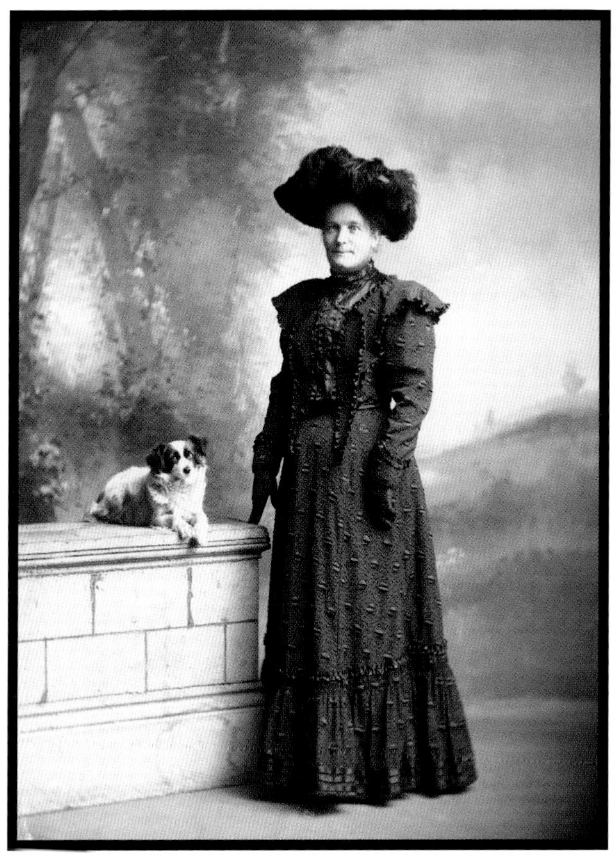

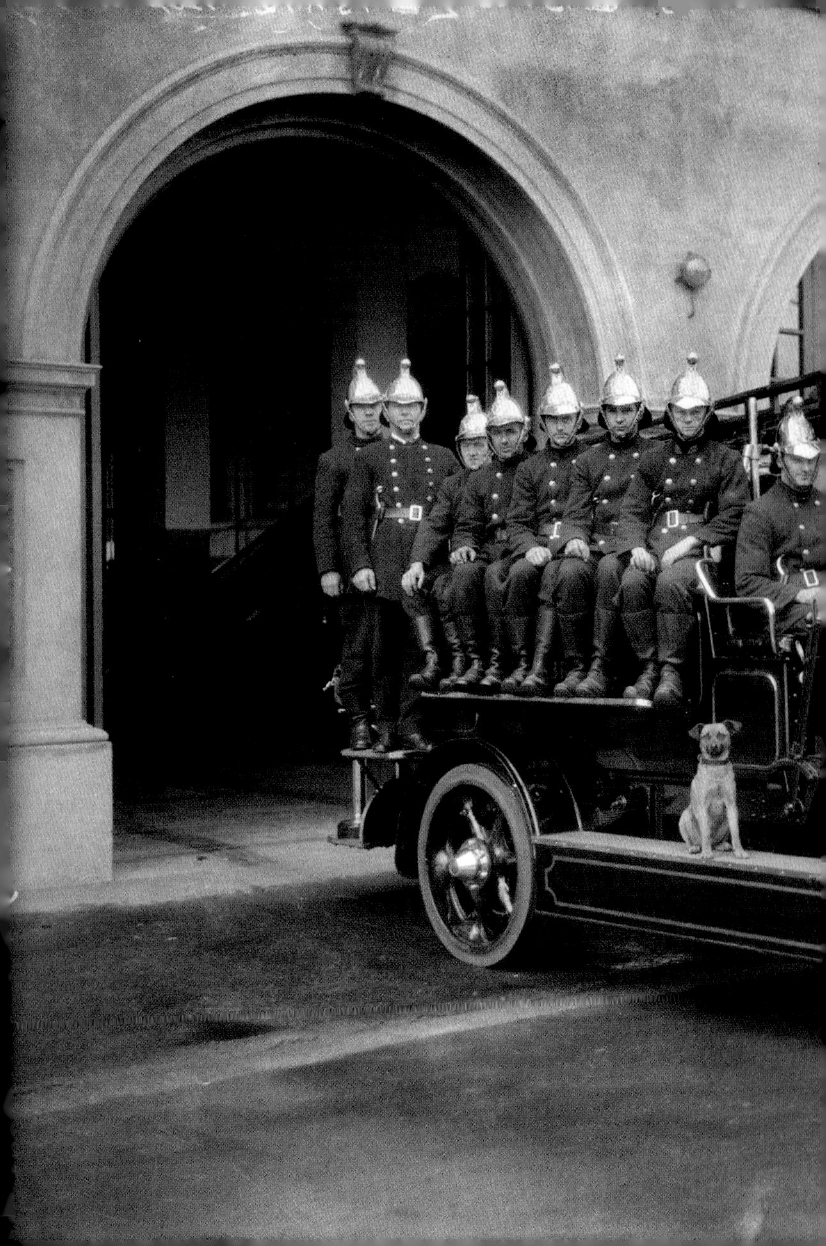

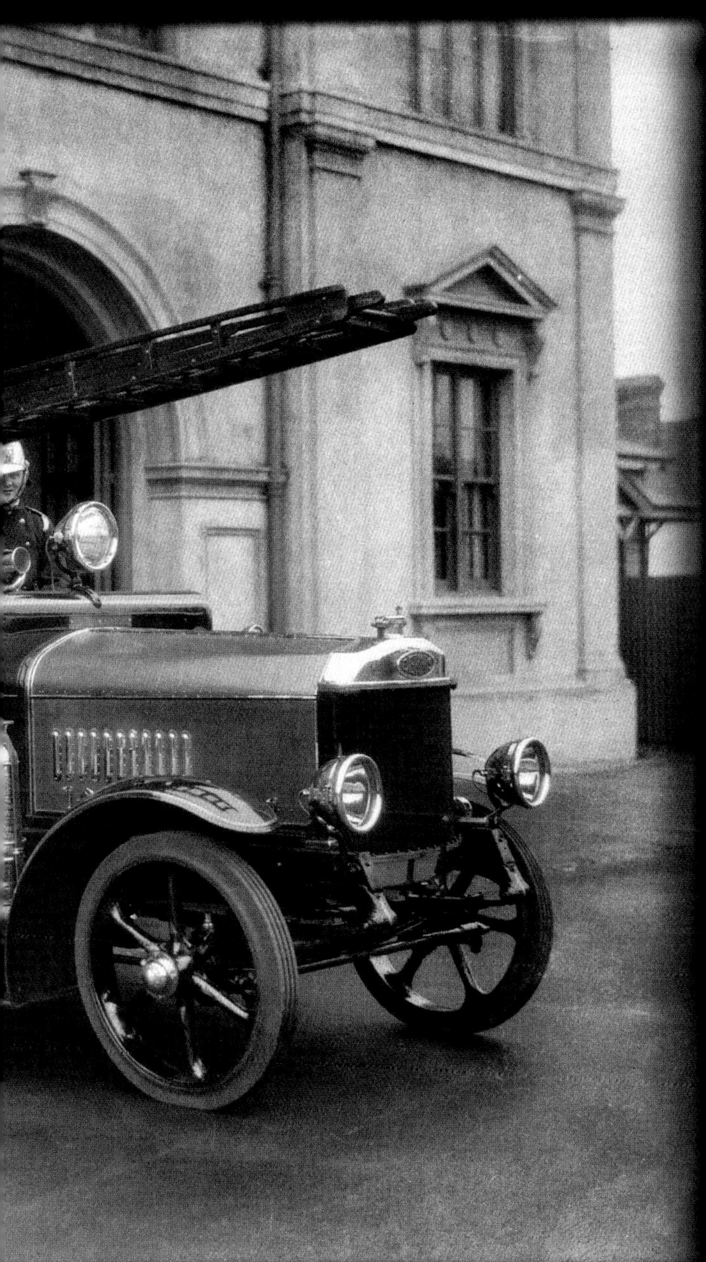

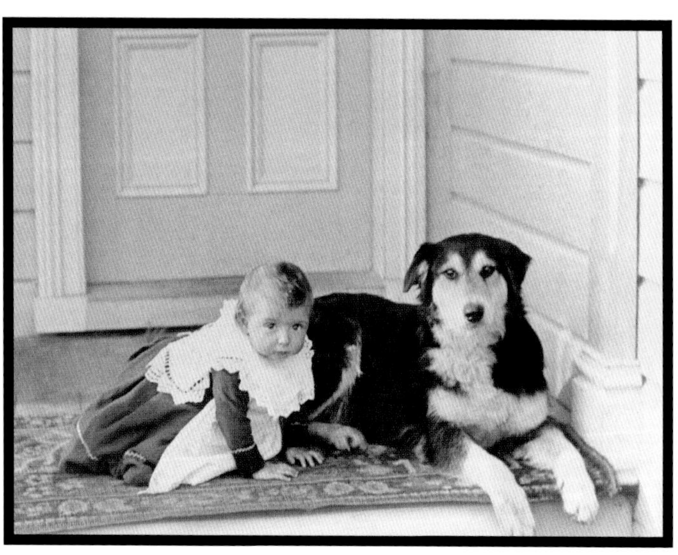

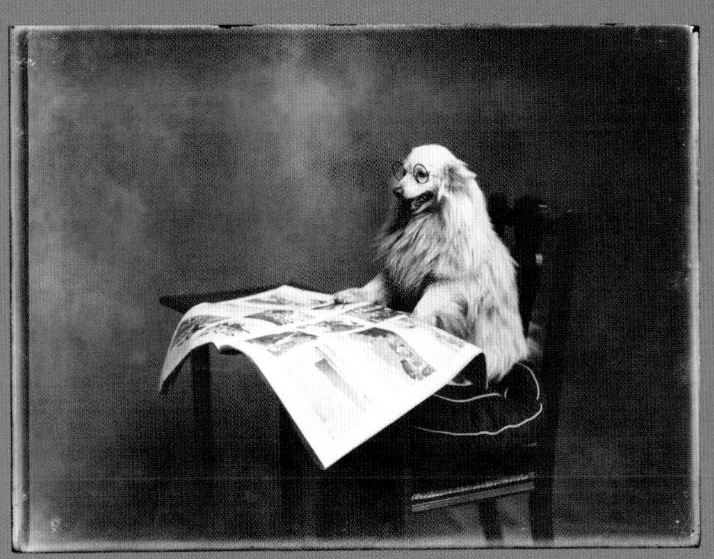

The Antarctic dog

In the summer of 1911, fourteen Siberian huskies were brought to Quail Island in Lyttelton Harbour for training. They were relief dogs destined to join Robert Falcon Scott's *Terra Nova* expedition, which was already on the ice. For a month, Yellow Belly, Snowy, Cheeky and the other dogs were exercised daily with a small makeshift sledge equipped with wheels. Excited to run, the dogs pulled fiercely and wildly and showed little regard for the human they were towing.

This photograph was taken by James Robert (Jim) Dennistoun (1883–1916). Born near Geraldine, in Canterbury, Dennistoun became a passionate mountain climber at a young age, and in 1911 was the first person to ascend Rahotu Mitre Peak. That same year, he was recruited as a volunteer on the *Terra Nova* expedition to look after seven stubborn Indian Army mules and these energetic Siberian sledge dogs. The animals were taken down to the ice in case Scott needed them for a second attempt at the South Pole. When Scott and his team died on their return from the first attempt, the mules and dogs were instead used by the parties that searched for their bodies.

Dennistoun served with the Royal Flying Corps in the First World War. He was shot down over France and died of his wounds in a German hospital in 1916. He had recorded his Antarctica trip in several photograph albums, which are now in the collection of Canterbury Museum.

For more about one of the dogs from the *Terra Nova* expedition, see page 90.

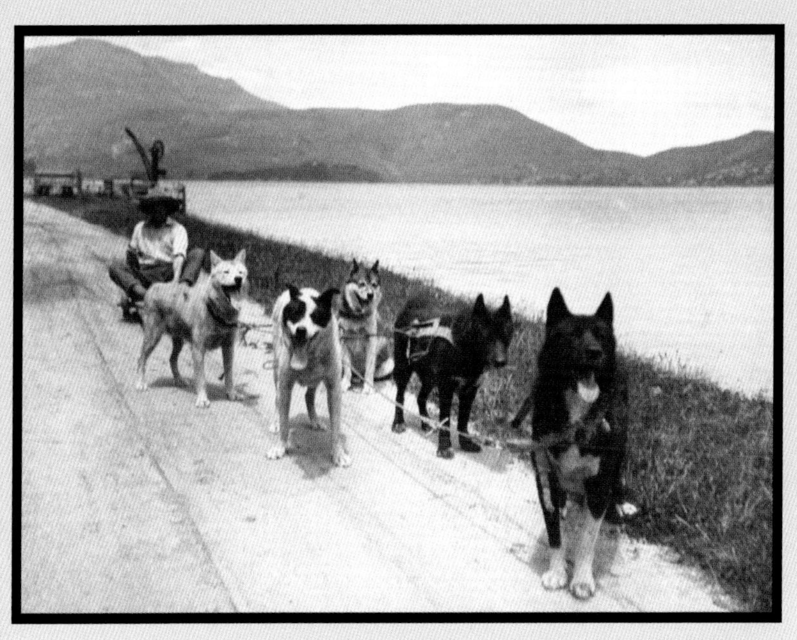

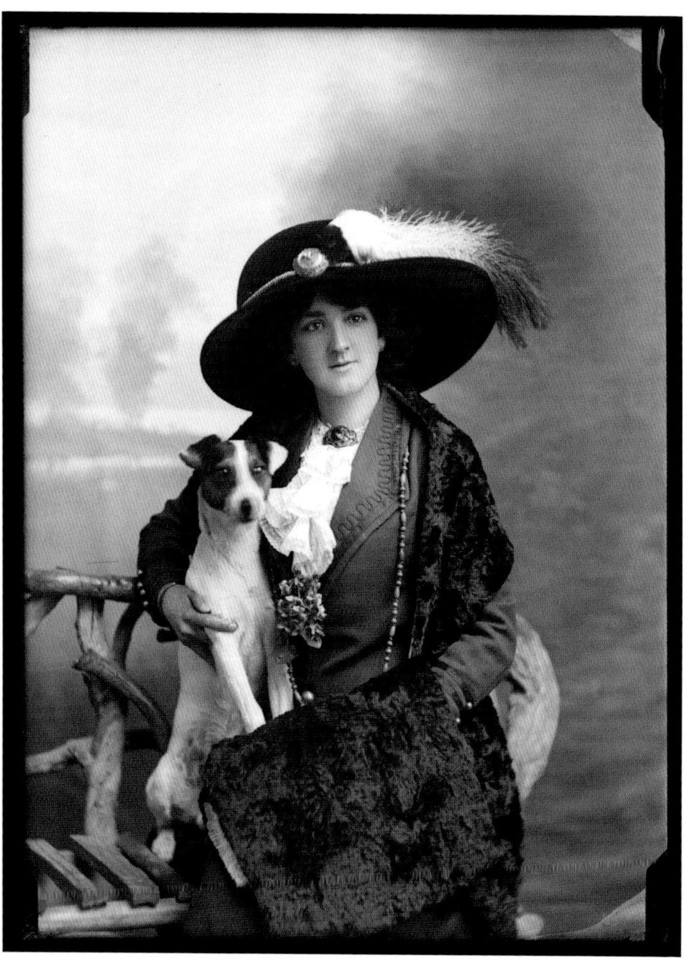

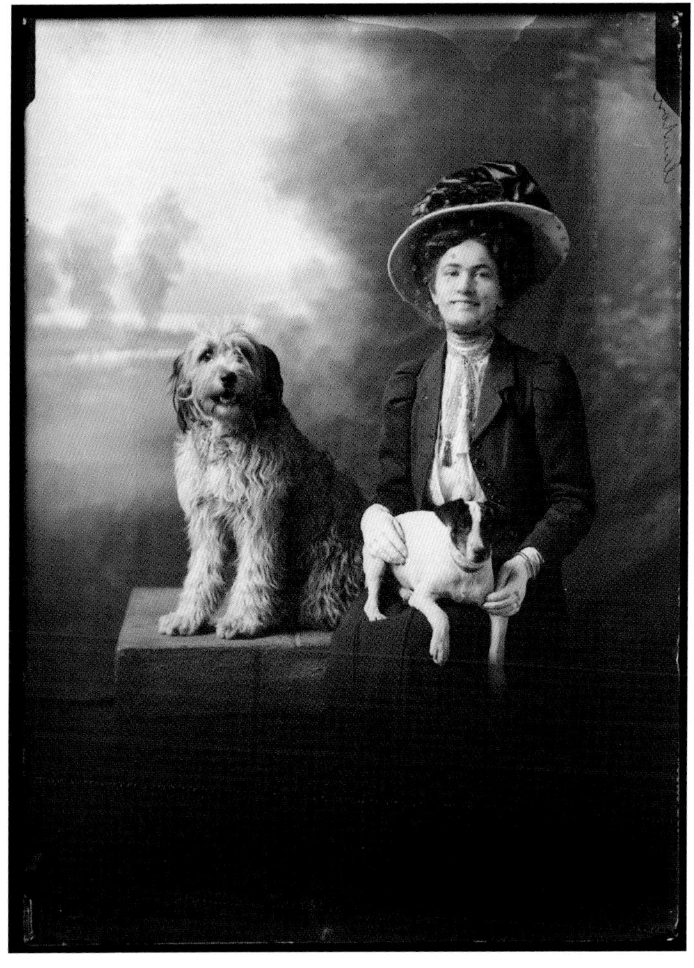

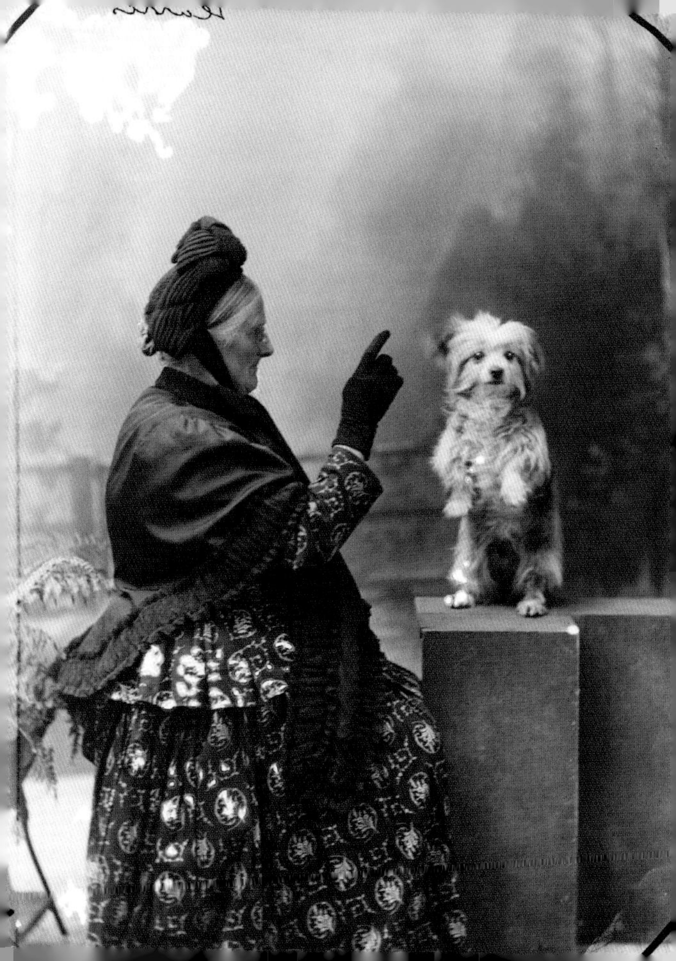

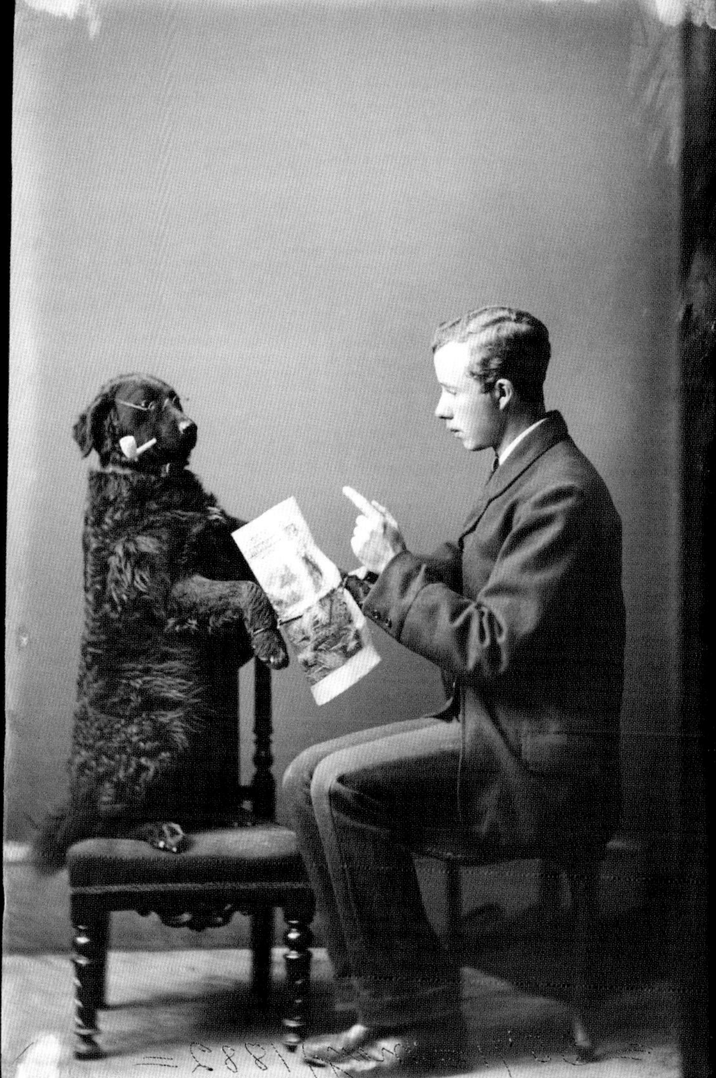

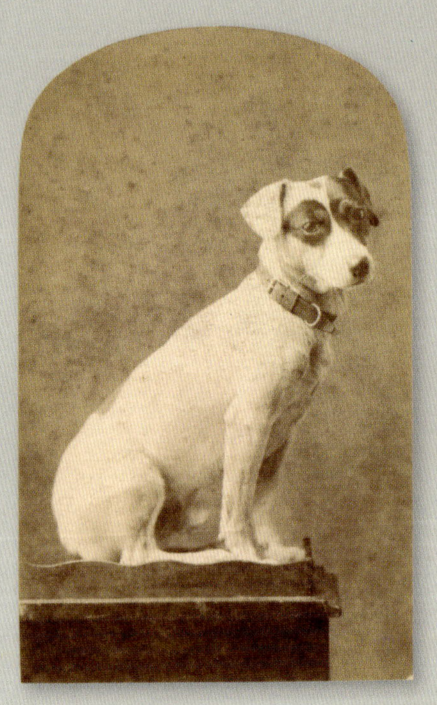

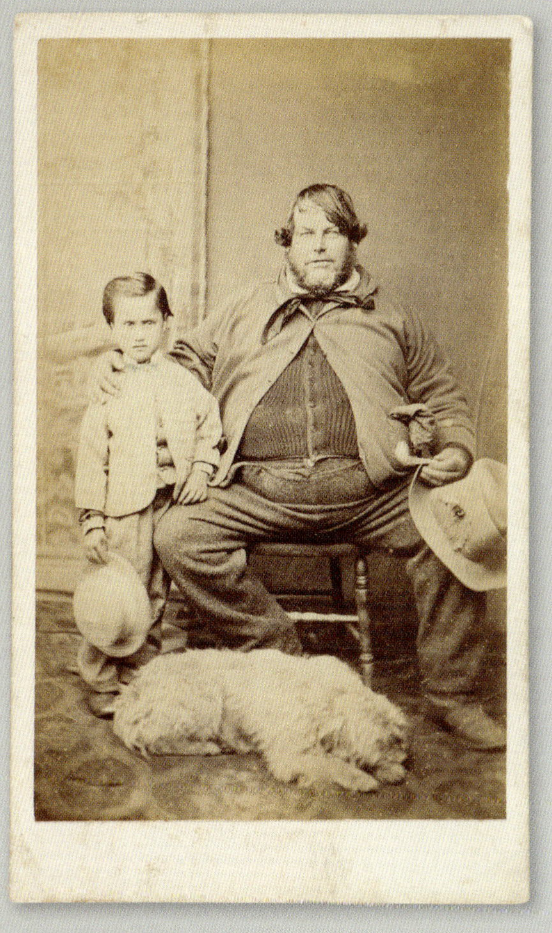

The Subantarctic islands dog

Remote and stormy Motu Ihupuku Campbell Island is the most southerly of the five groups of New Zealand's Subantarctic Islands to the south and east of the South Island, in New Zealand territorial waters. It is buffeted by the Roaring Forties and Fifties and its climate is, in a word, challenging: winds of over 60 kilometres an hour for 280 days a year, rain for 300 days each year, sunshine hours of only 660 each year, and a mean average temperature of 7°C. Although the soils are acidic, it was nonetheless considered suitable for farming by the government, which in 1894 auctioned off the pastoral lease to Run Number 511.

In 1904, fourteen farmers from the Shetland Islands, their working dogs and a boatload of sheep arrived on the 113-square-metre island to manage the farm for the leaseholder, George Tucker, who had taken over the lease in 1900. Their task was to farm in the summer and hunt whales in the winter. This photo from 1904 shows, from left to right, Peter Williamson, Adam Adamson, Frank Manson, A. Nicolson and two unnamed Border collies.

Prior to the Shetlanders' arrival, human occupation of the island had been limited to occasional visits by Māori, sealers and whalers, scientists and castaways. Ships had brought rats, which wiped out the land birds, and now large numbers of sheep were set to further upset the unique mega-herb ecosystem.

It was tough going, and the ships that would bring in supplies and take off wool came infrequently. Eventually even the doughty Shetland Islanders found the place too tough; they were but the first to bail. The run was finally abandoned by the last leaseholder in 1931. The Department of Conservation began systematically eradicating feral sheep, cats and rats from the 1990s. The island was declared rat-free in 2001 and the unique ecosystem is now recovering.

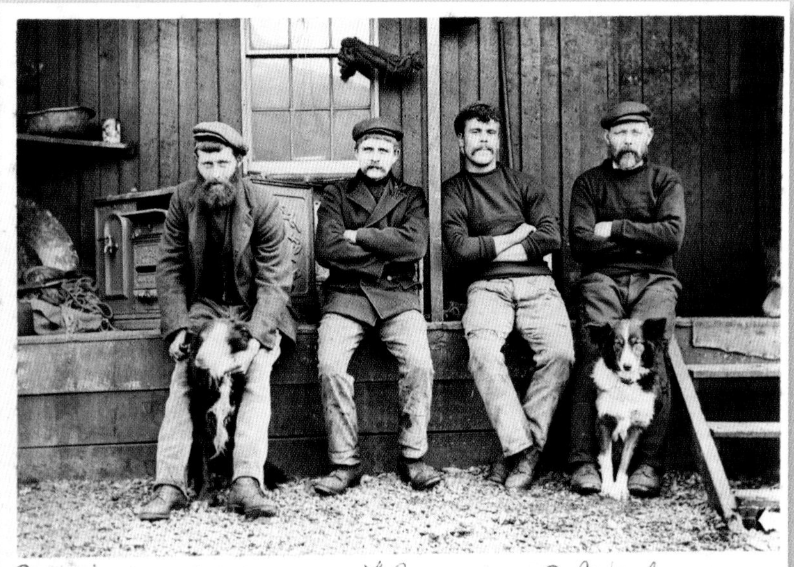

P. Williamson A Adamson Jas Manson A Nicolson
First men to take sheep to Campbell Islands
all Shetland Islanders

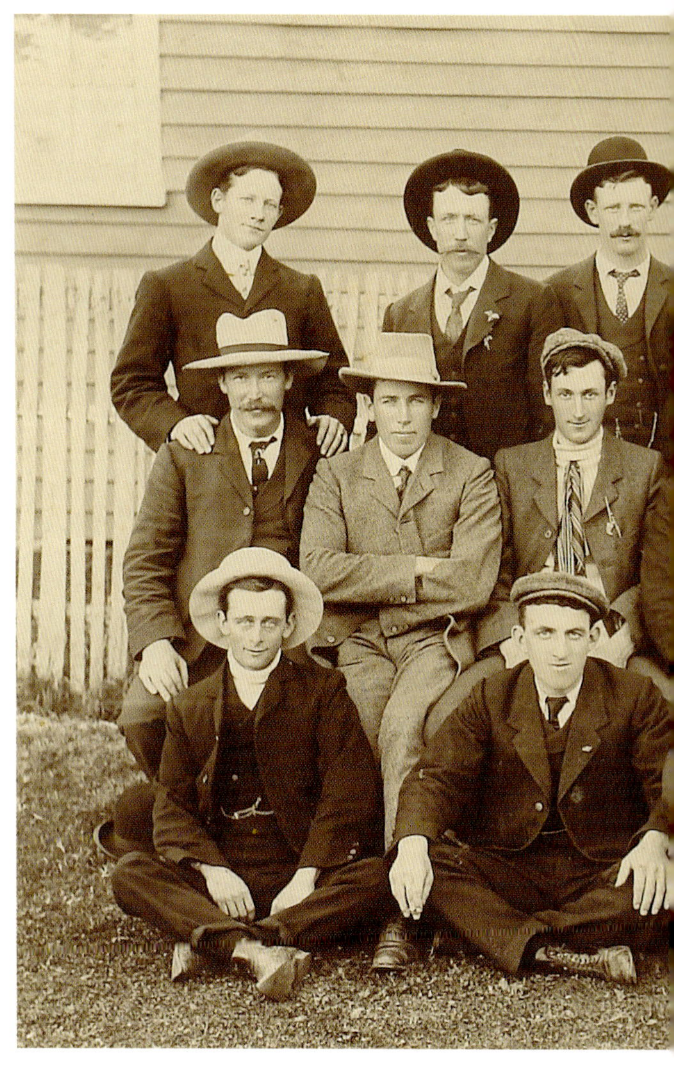

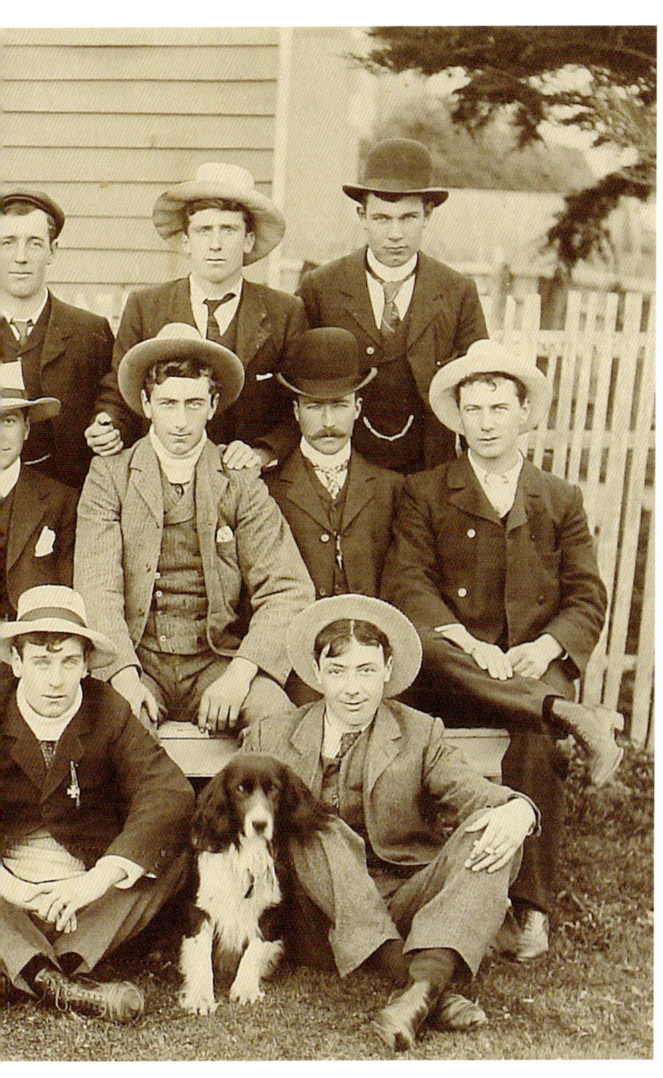

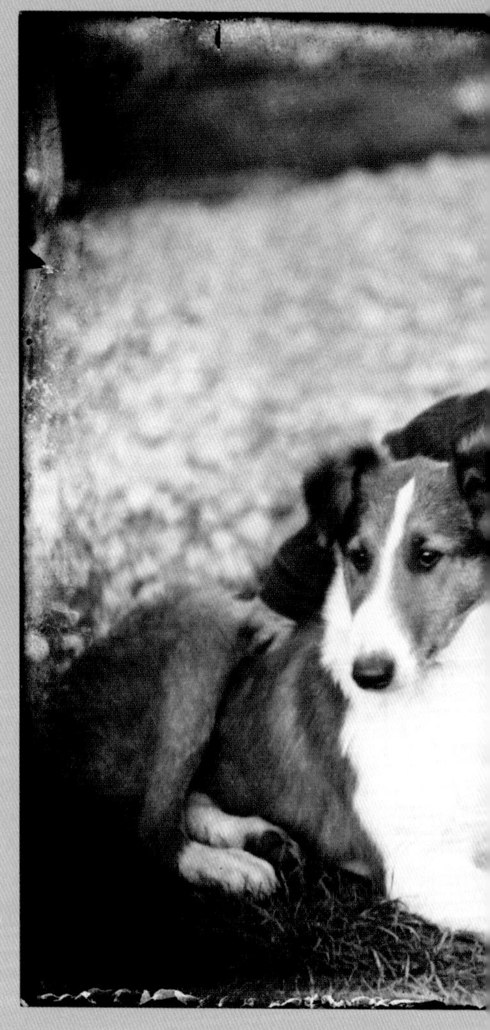

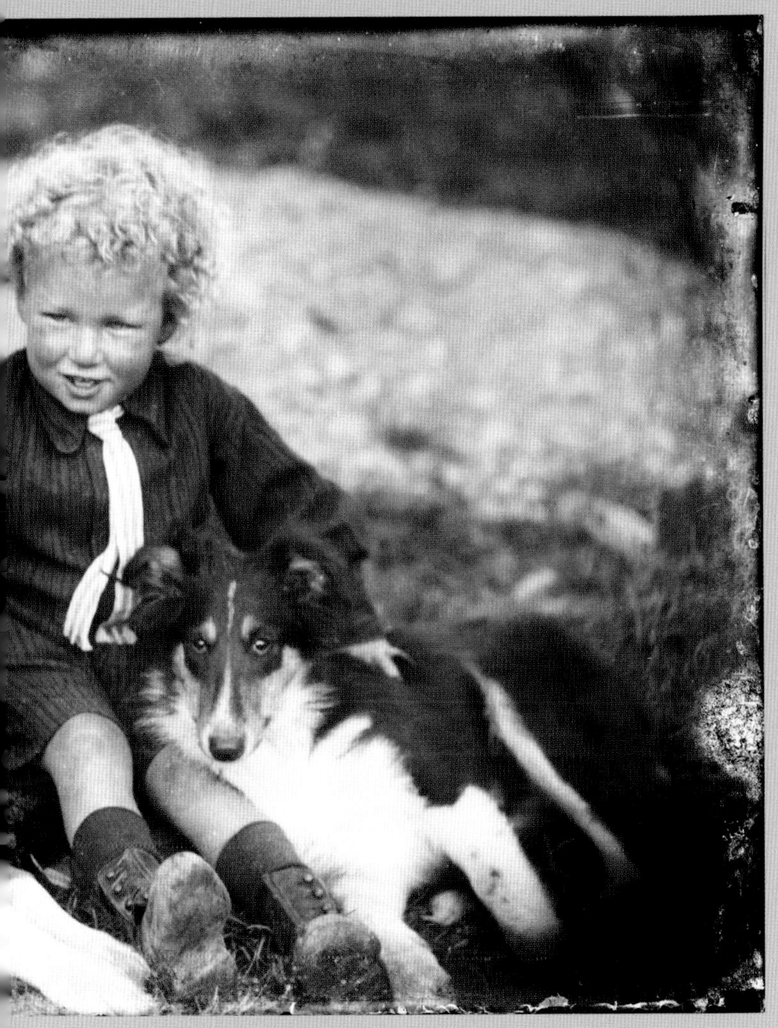

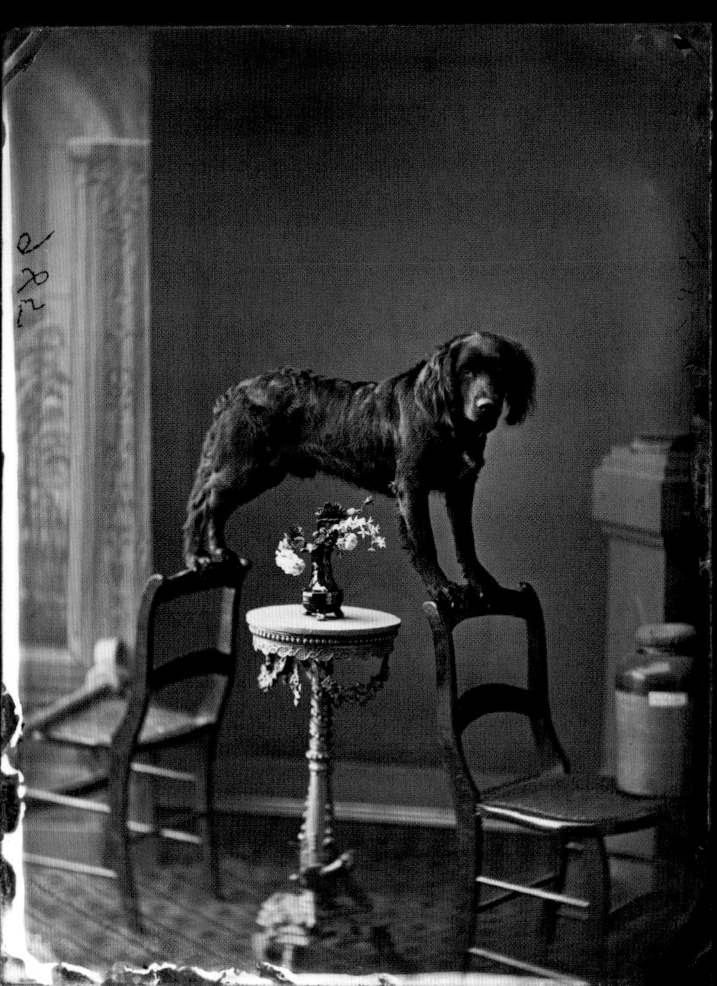

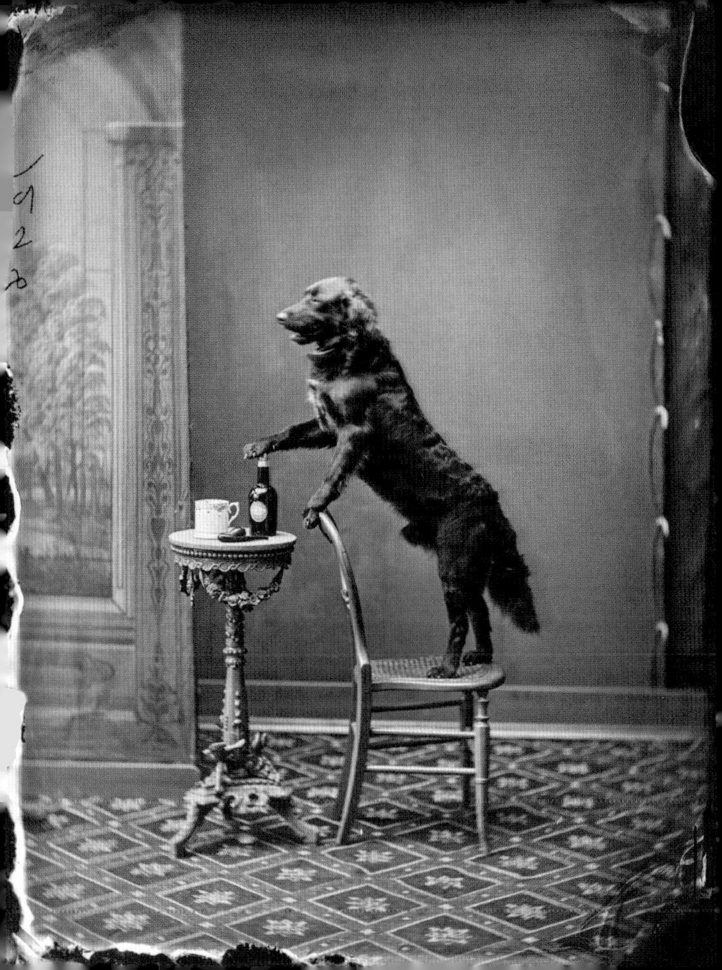

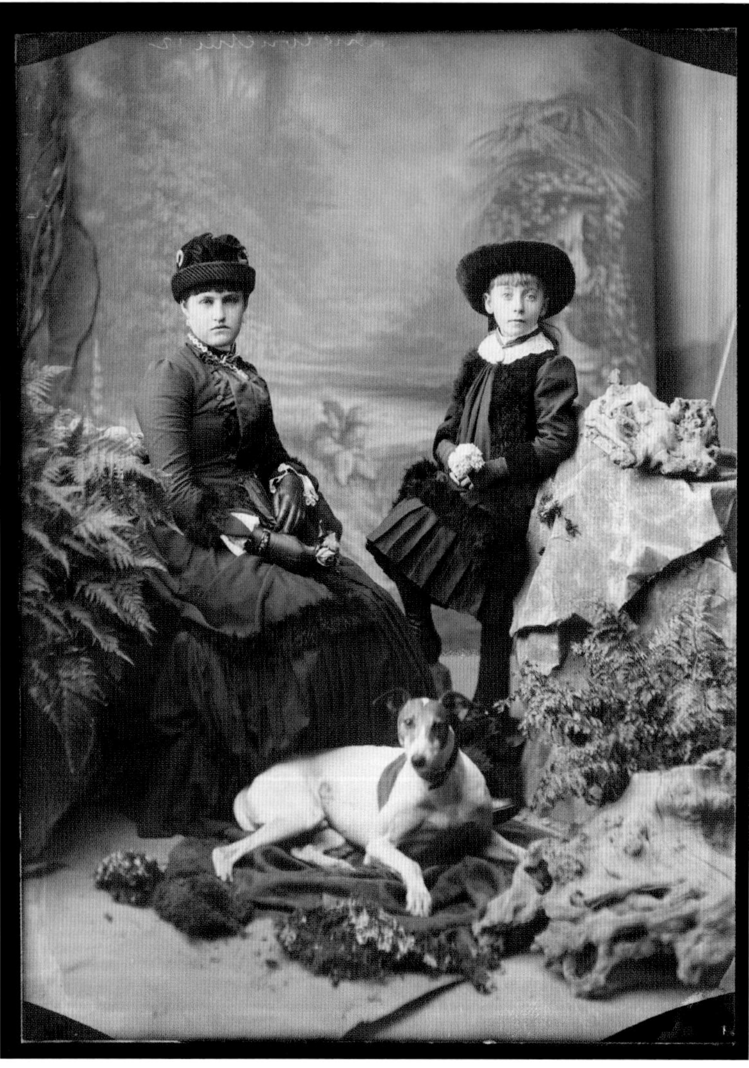

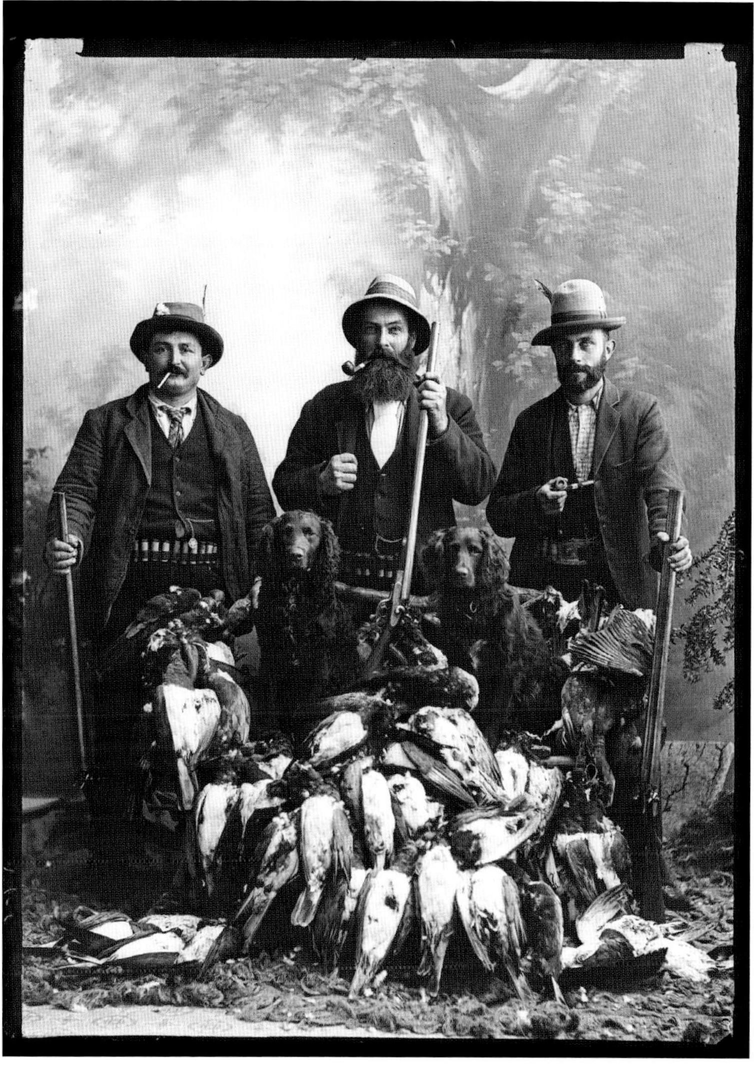

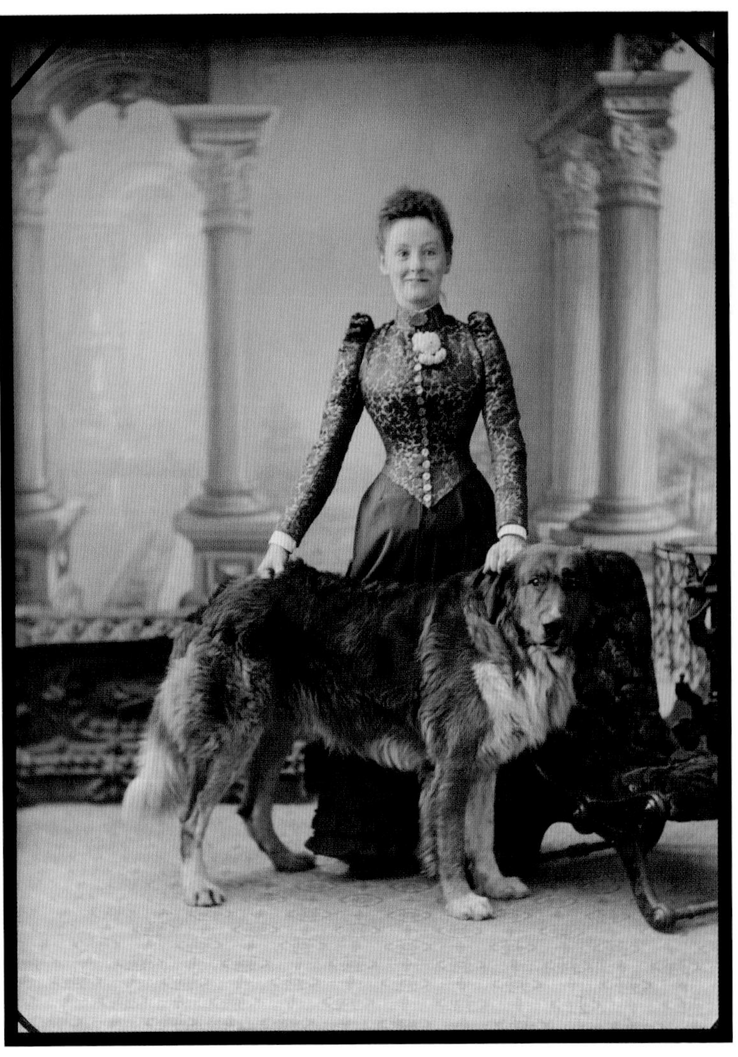

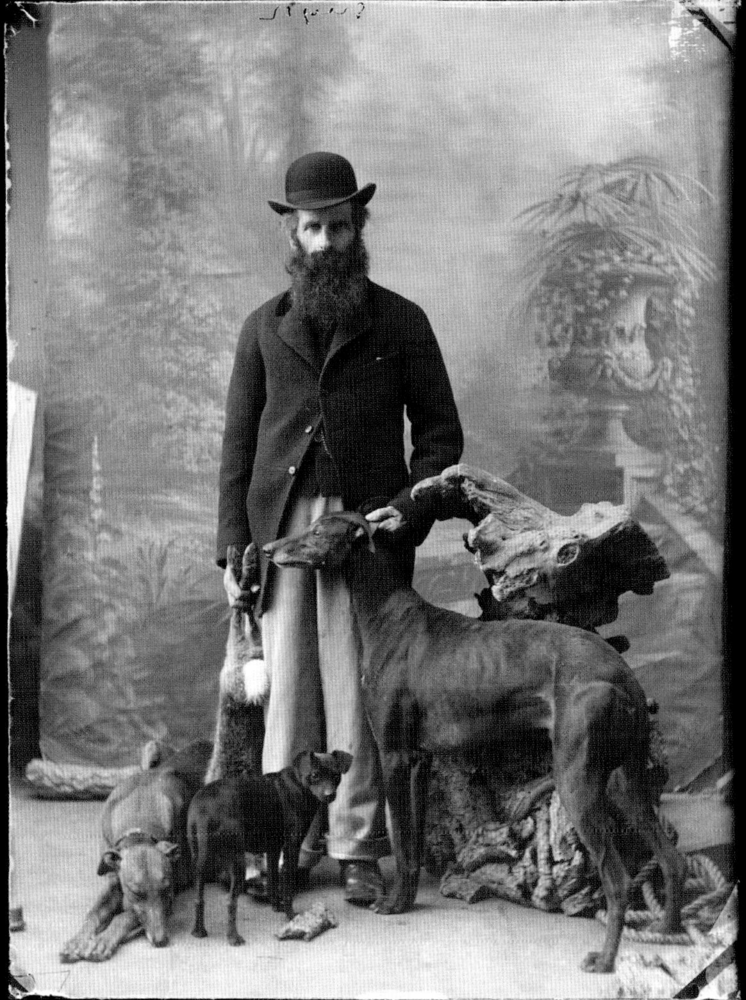

The explorer's dog

This photograph of the inveterate explorer Charles Douglas (1840–1916) and his dog Betsey Jane was taken around 1894, by which time he was towards the end of his forty years of exploring the South Island.

Douglas arrived in New Zealand from Scotland in 1862, aged twenty-two, and quickly exchanged his Edinburgh life in a bank for shepherding, goldmining and droving. In 1868 he accompanied geologist and Canterbury Museum founder Julius von Haast into southern Westland, and from that time his interest in geology, flora and fauna drove a life of independent exploration and surveying.

His maps and recordings of plant and bird life were of great value to the government, and in 1889 he was finally put on the payroll of the Survey Department, which occasionally referred to him in its official reports as 'Mr Explorer Douglas'. His contribution to information on resources and routes was recognised with the Royal Geographical Society's Gill Memorial Prize in 1897.

Douglas lived simply and frugally, hunting and fishing and occasionally picking up work droving for extra money. He was accompanied on his often dangerous explorations of some of the most rugged terrain in New Zealand by a dog. For many years it was Topsy; his last canine companion was the Border collie Betsey Jane.

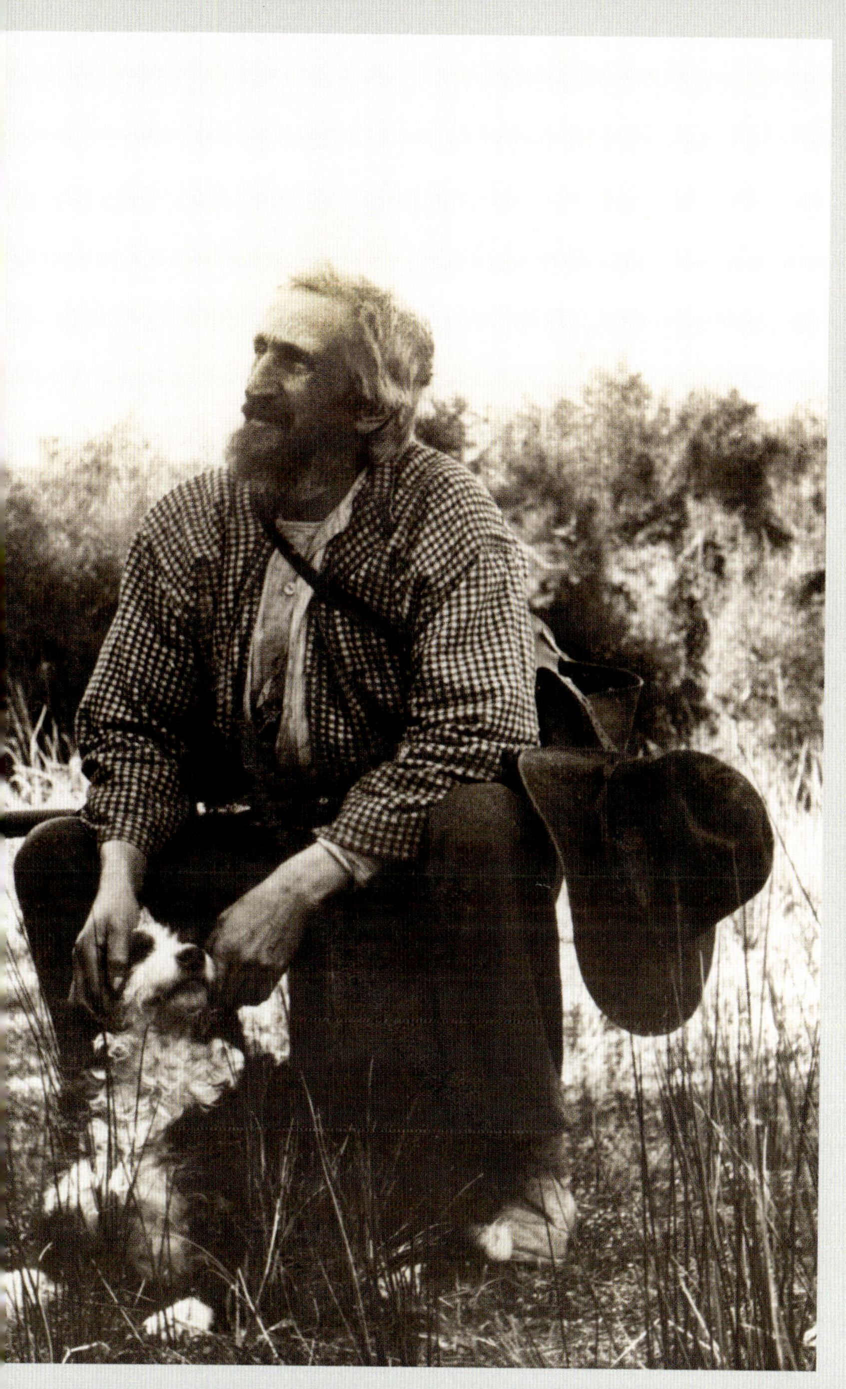

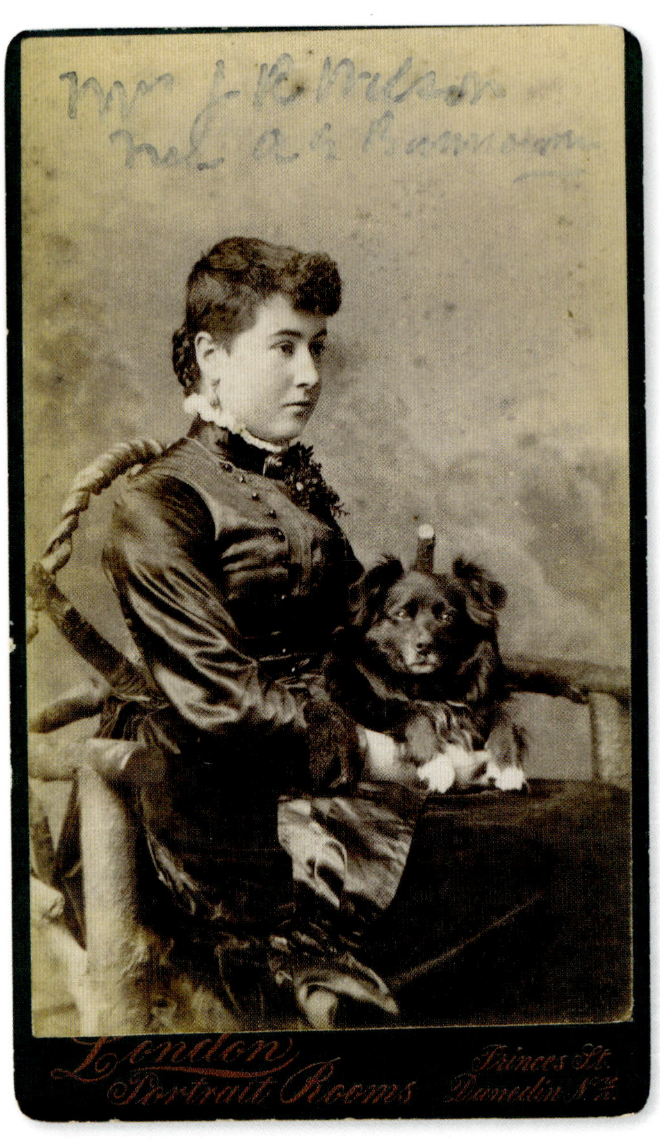
London
Portrait Rooms
Princes St.
Dunedin N.Z.

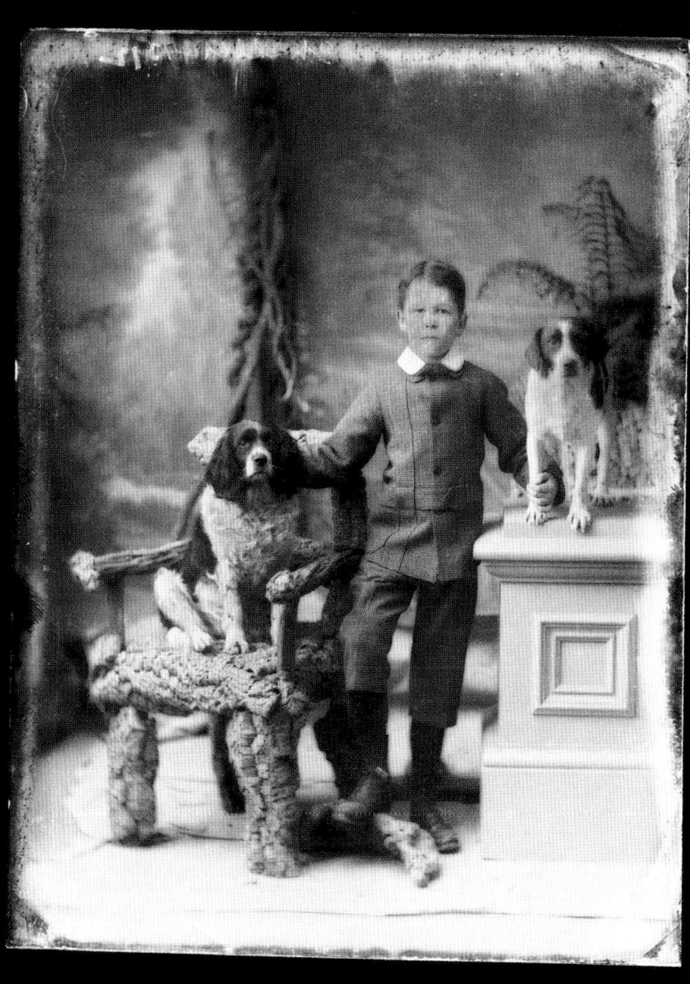

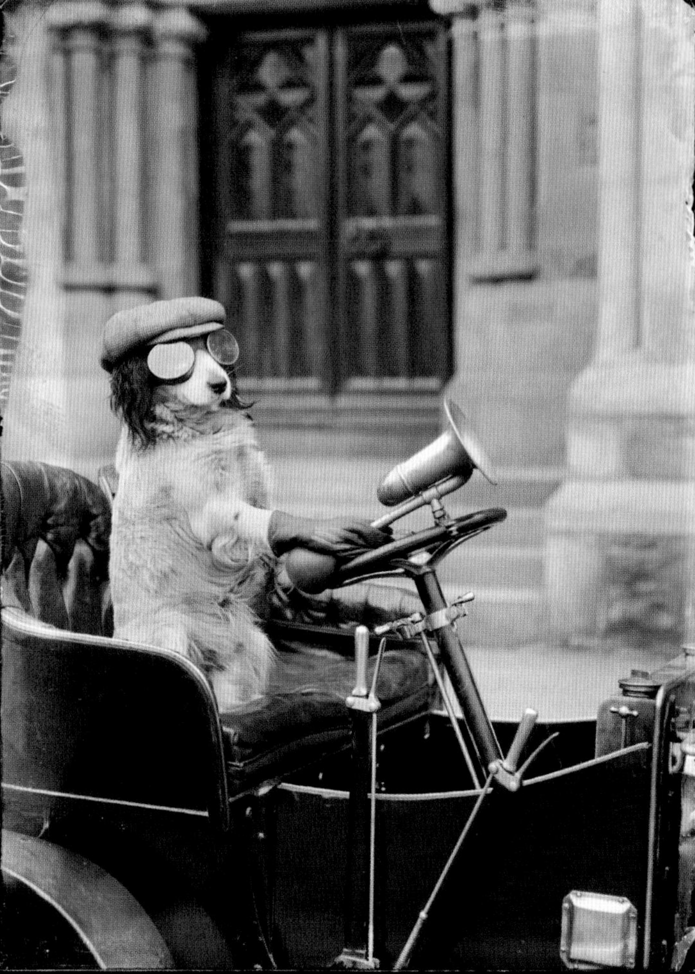

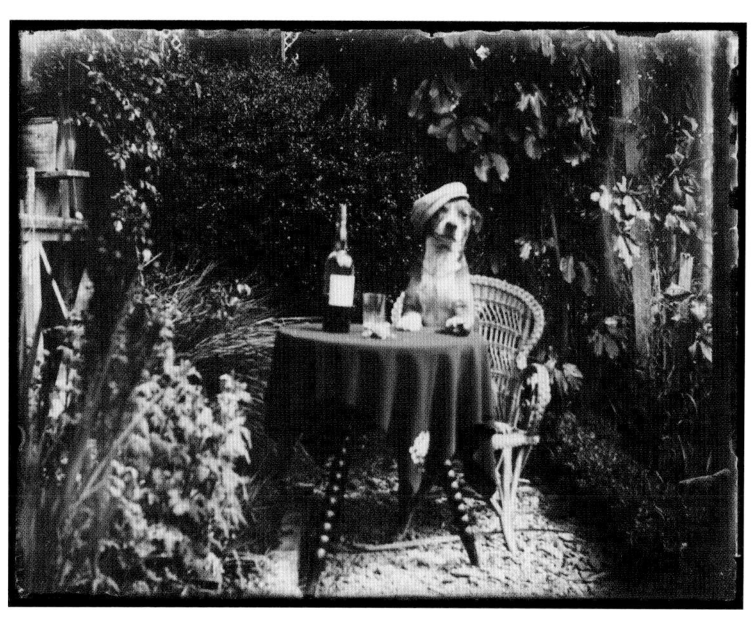

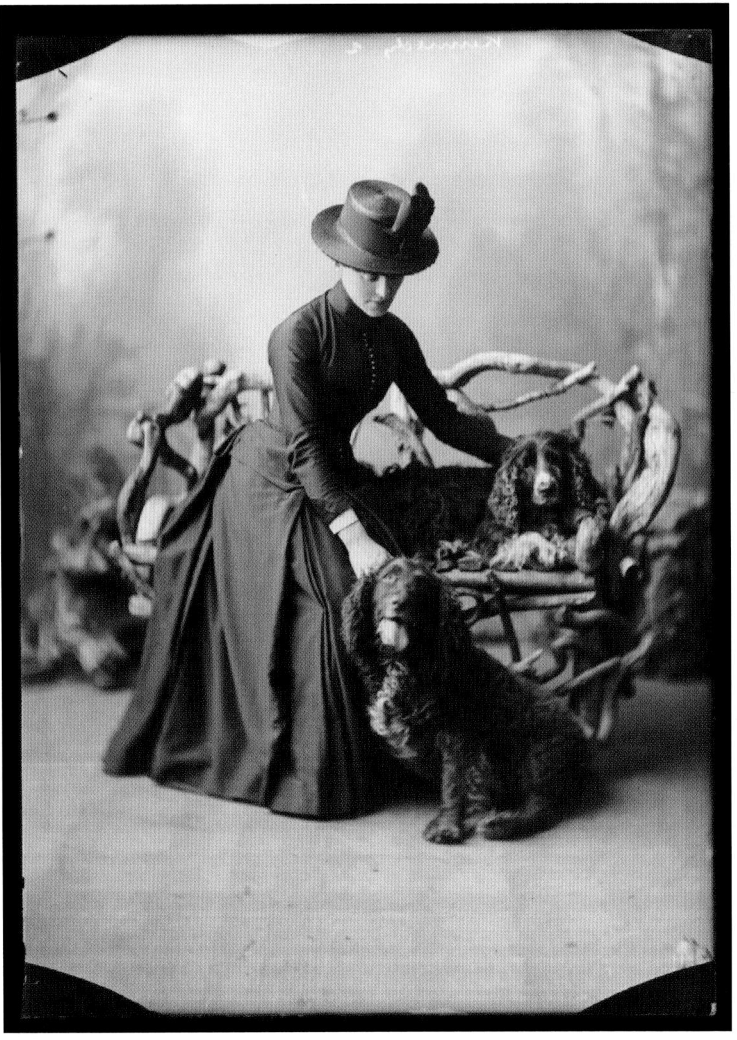

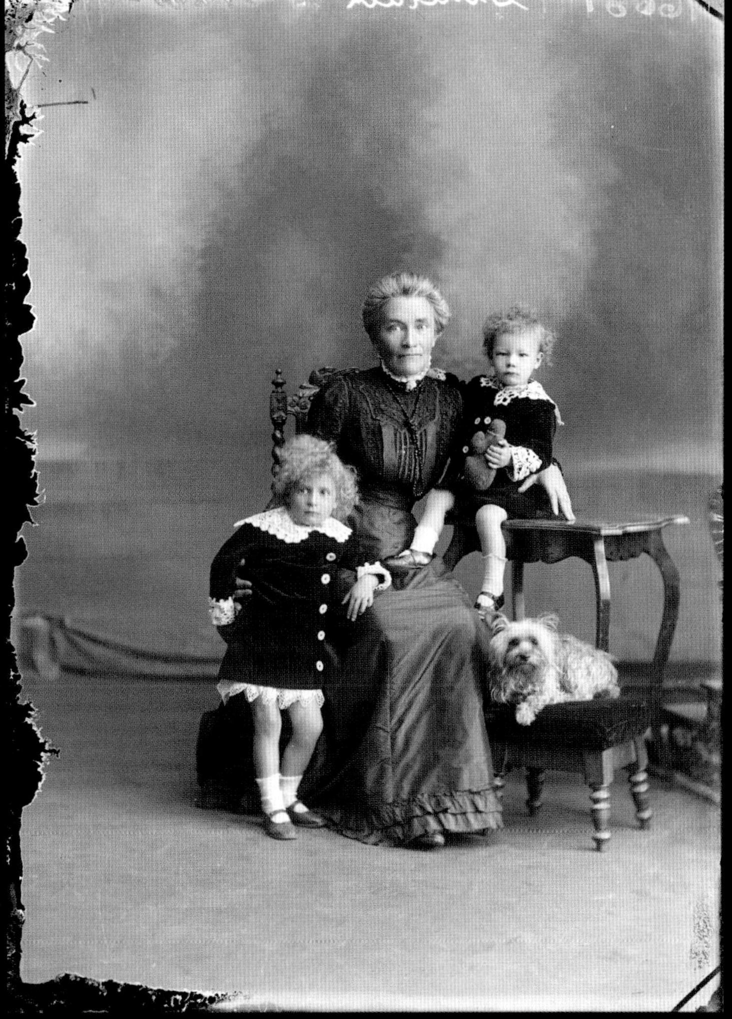

The match-making dog

This photograph of Erebus and his owner Beatrice Curlett of Christchurch was taken in 1909. Erebus was one of the thirteen pups born on the Antarctic ice during the British Antarctic Expedition to the South Pole led by Ernest Shackleton. His parents, whose names are unknown, were among the nine Samoyeds bred and trained on Rakiura Stewart Island and brought up to Lyttelton to spend time training on Quail Island before being taken on board the *Nimrod*. The ship was given a rousing send-off as it set sail for Ross Island in McMurdo Sound in January 1908.

Shackleton only got as far as the 88th parallel before calling the attempt on the Pole off. The *Nimrod* returned to Lyttelton in 1909 with Erebus, who had been named after the volcano which the expedition members had summited. The Samoyed was presented to Beatrice Curlett by crew member Ernest Joyce, who had been in charge of the expedition's dogs and sleds. The two exchanged letters for a while and then were reacquainted in 1917, when Joyce was back in Christchurch as part of Shackleton's Imperial Trans-Antarctic Expedition. During the trip, it is reported that Joyce spotted Erebus out for a walk and gave a food call from the days of the expedition. Erebus came bounding up to his old friend. Joyce and Beatrice married a year later, and their romance, enabled by their shared love of Erebus the Samoyed, made a splash in newspapers both here and in Britain.

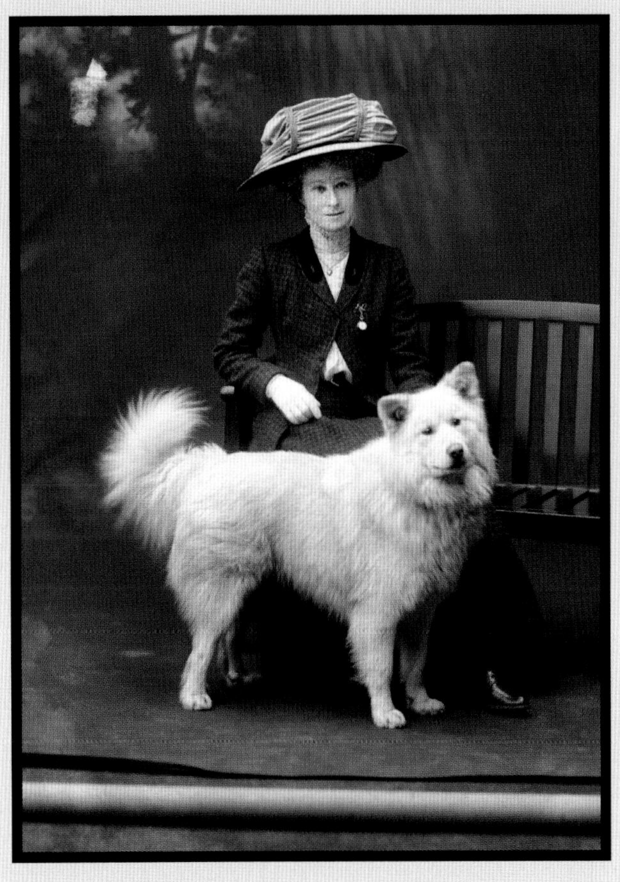

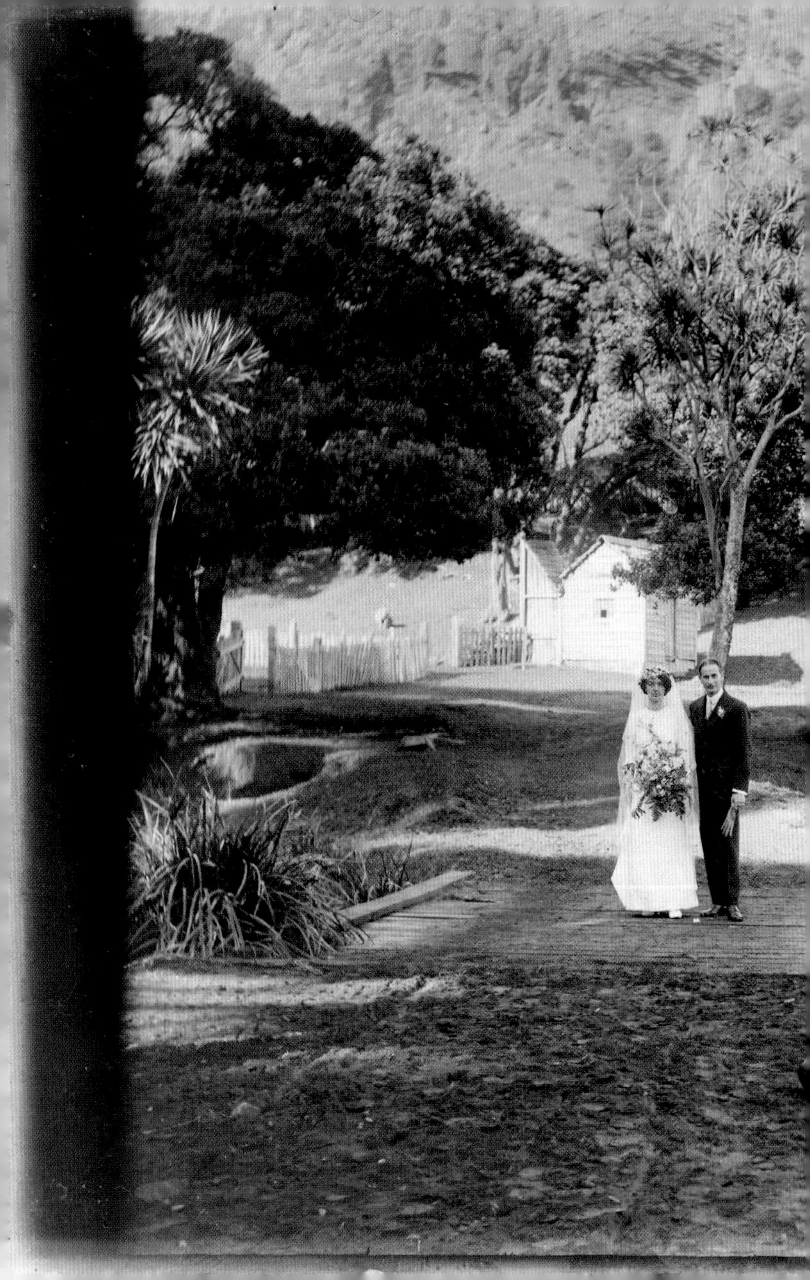

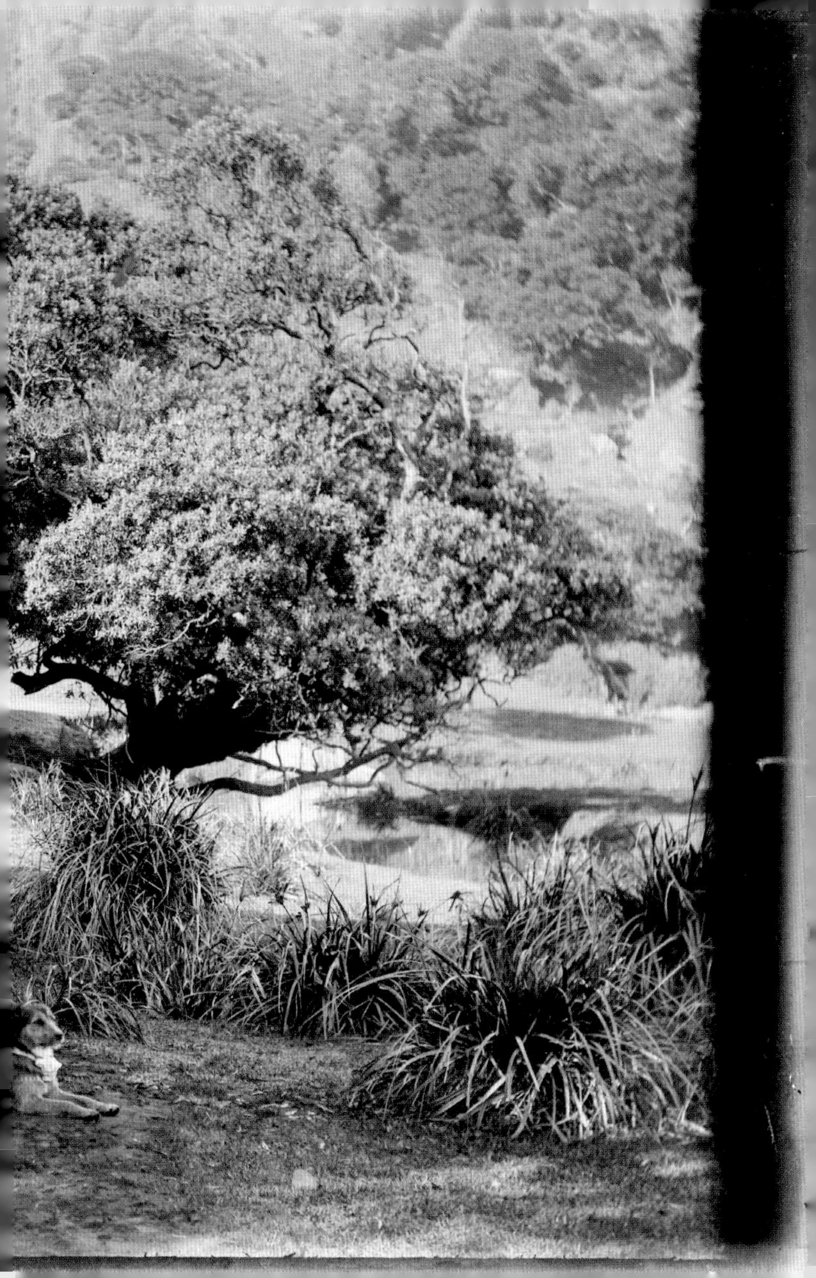

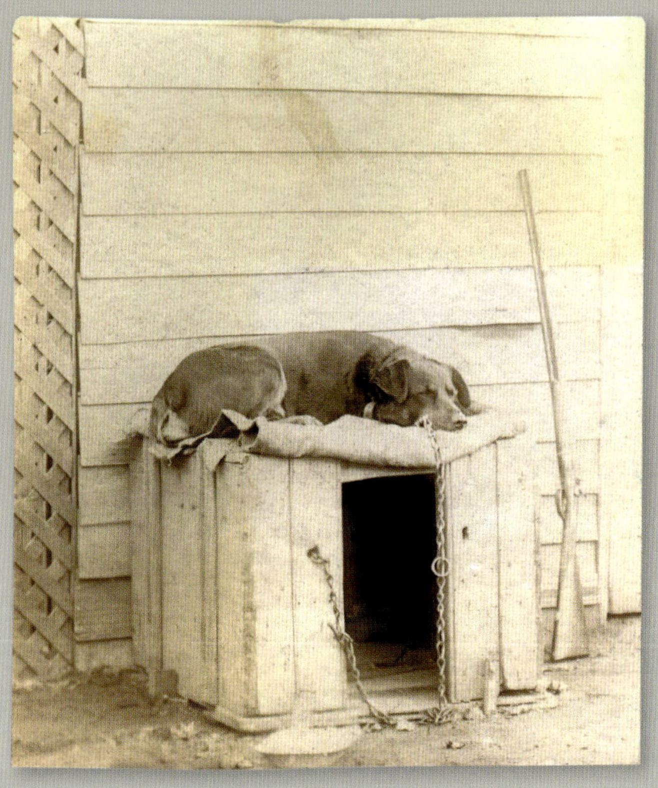

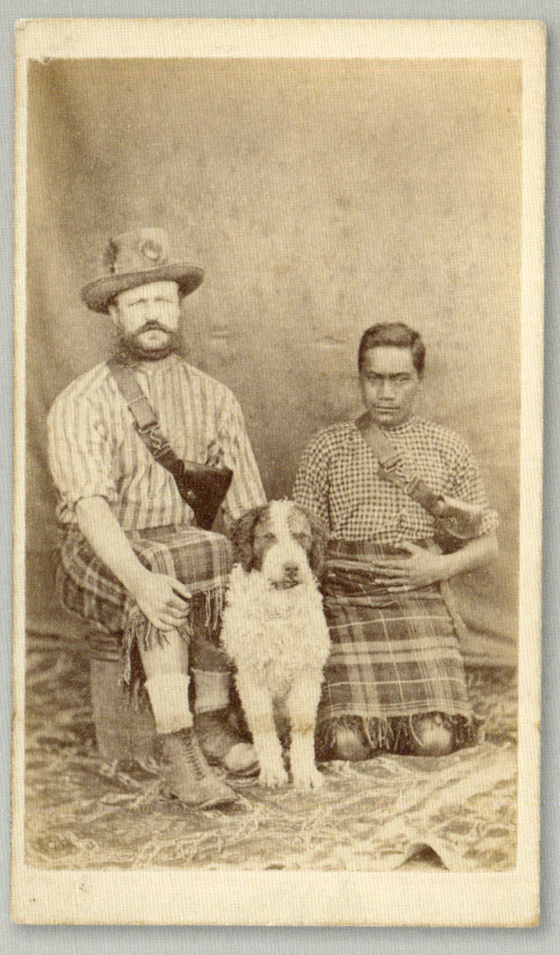

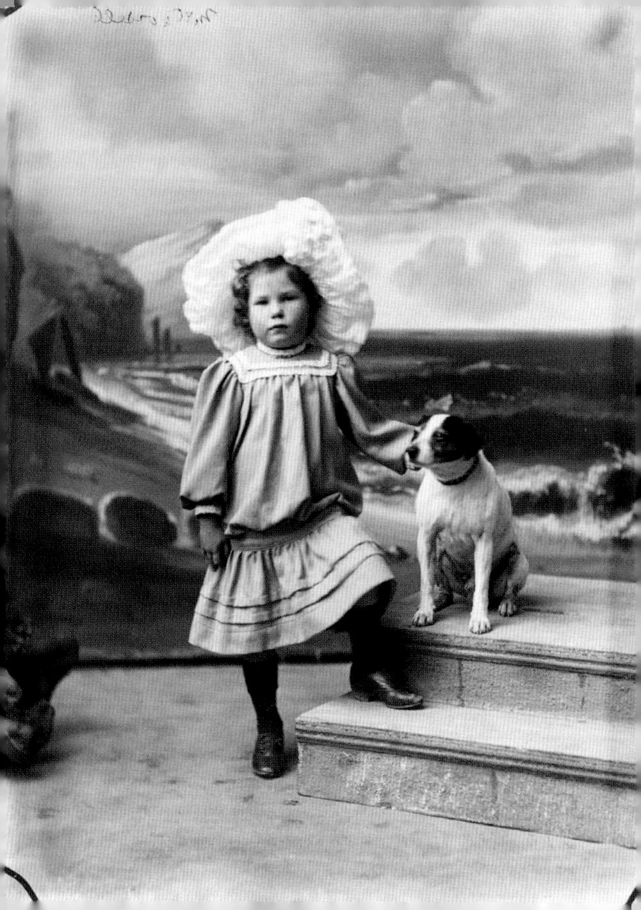

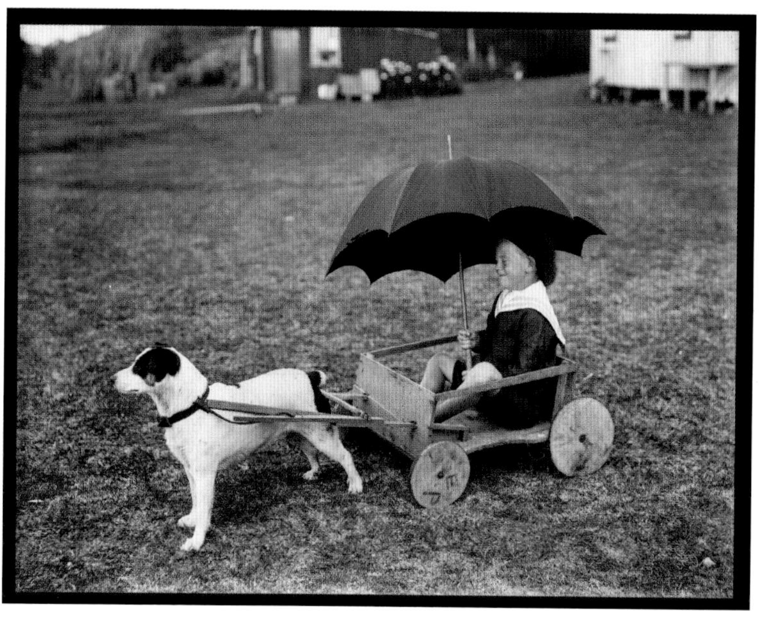

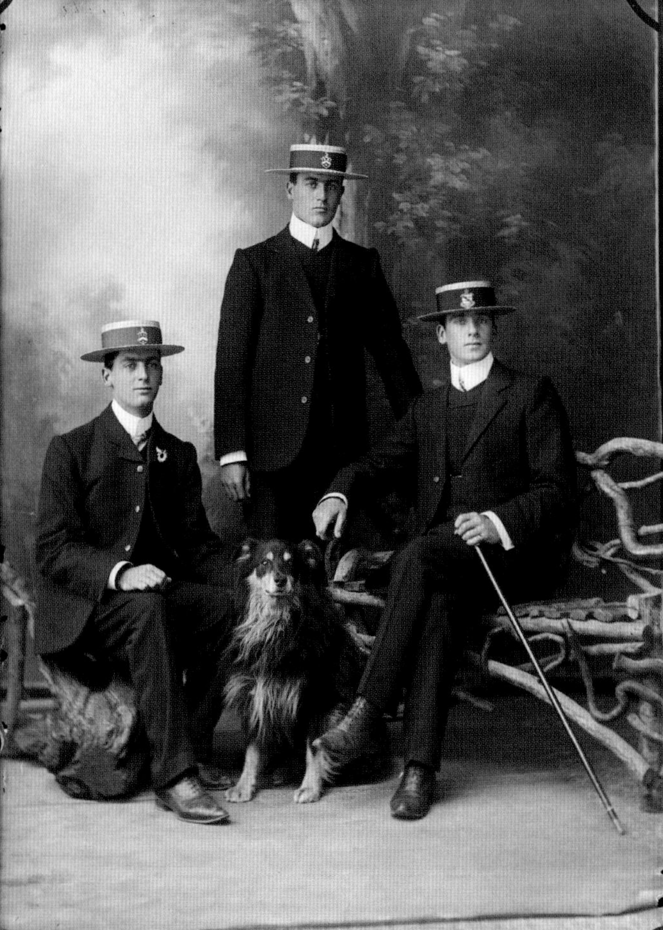

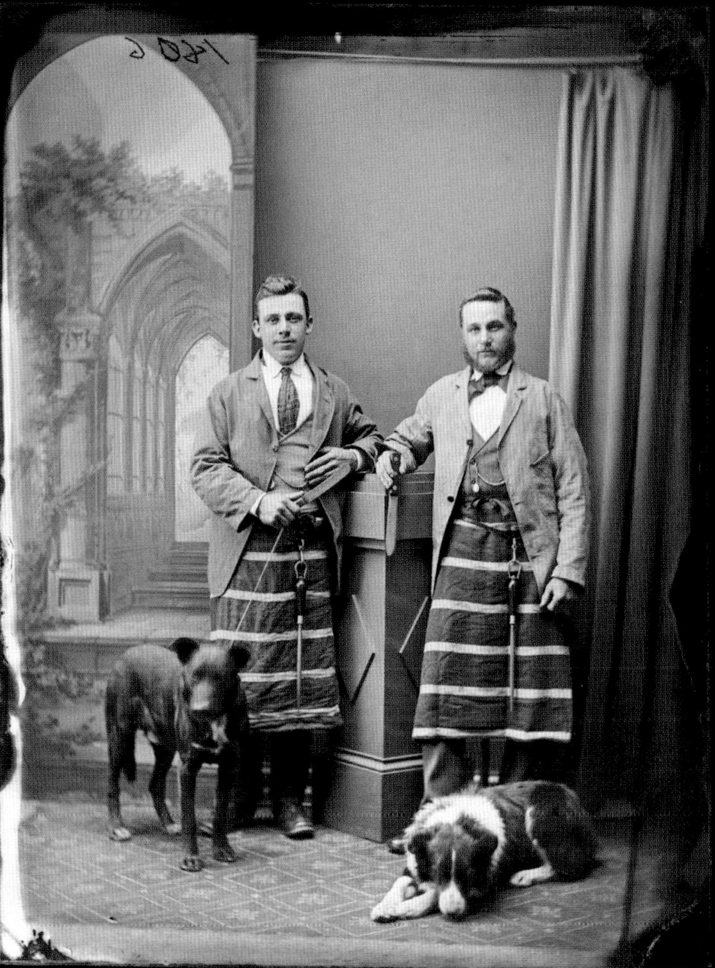

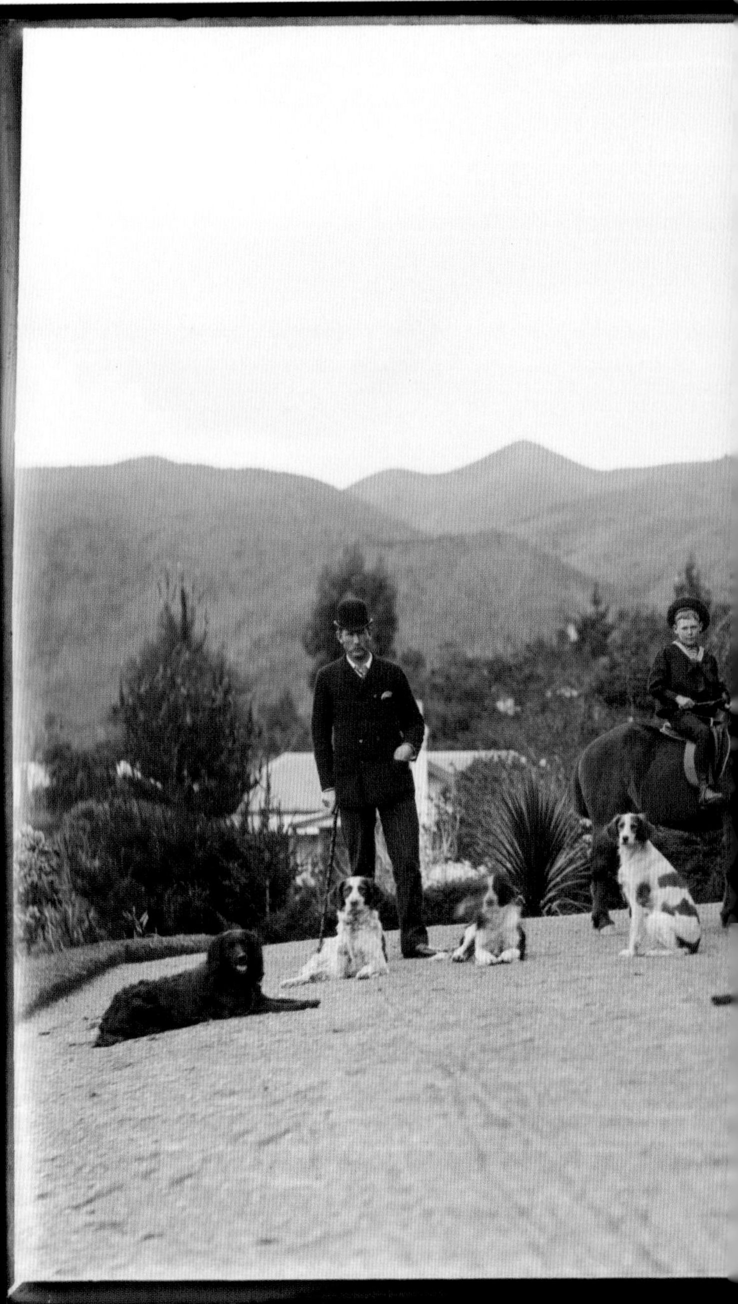

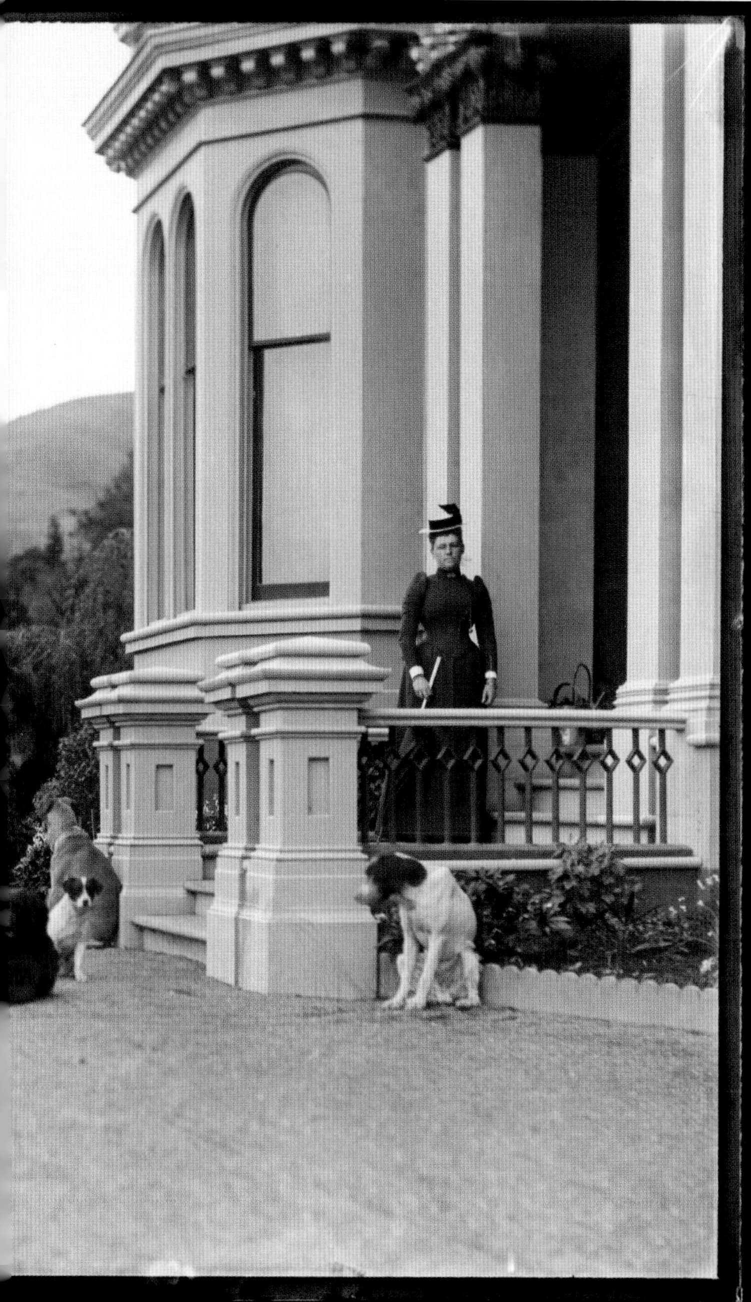

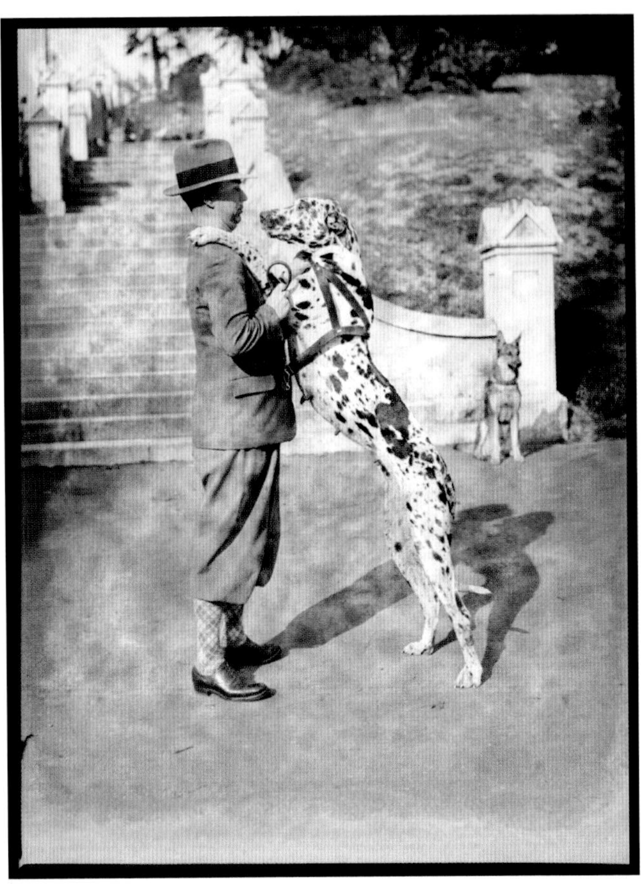

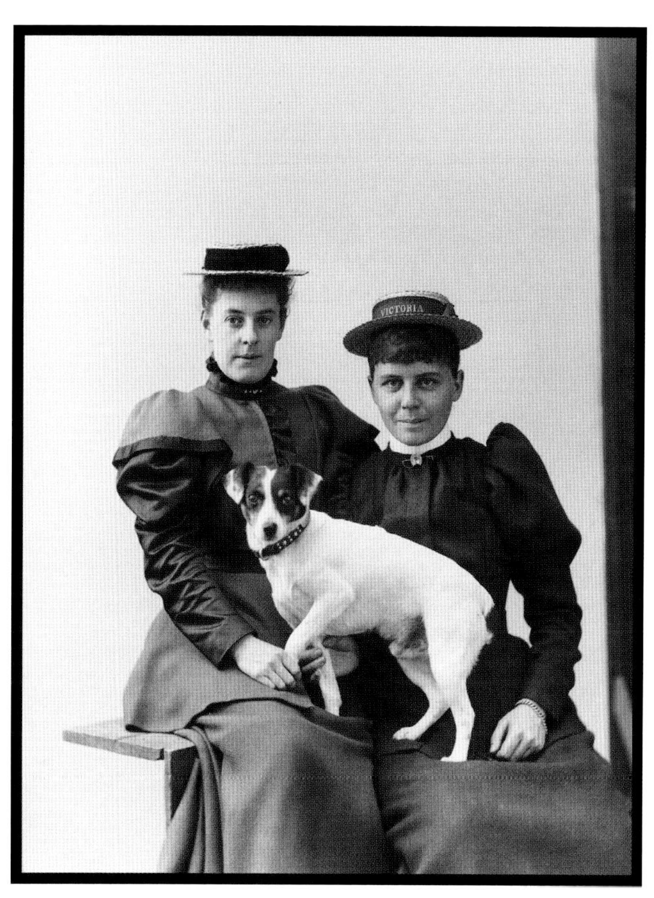
VICTORIA

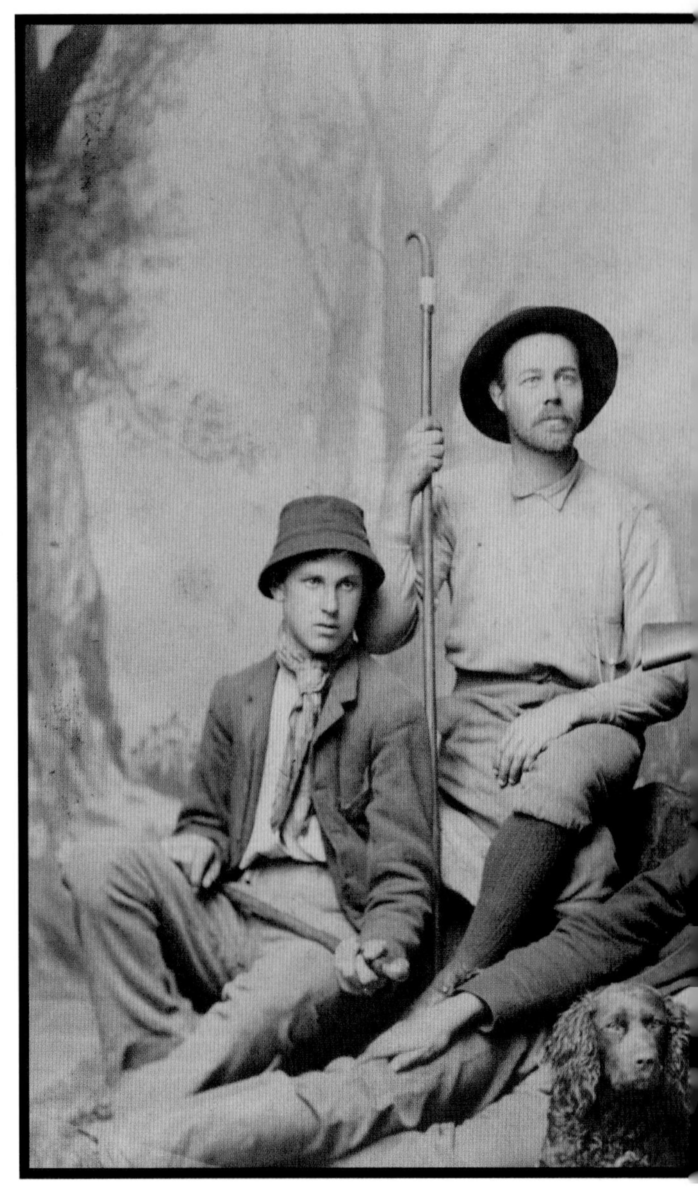

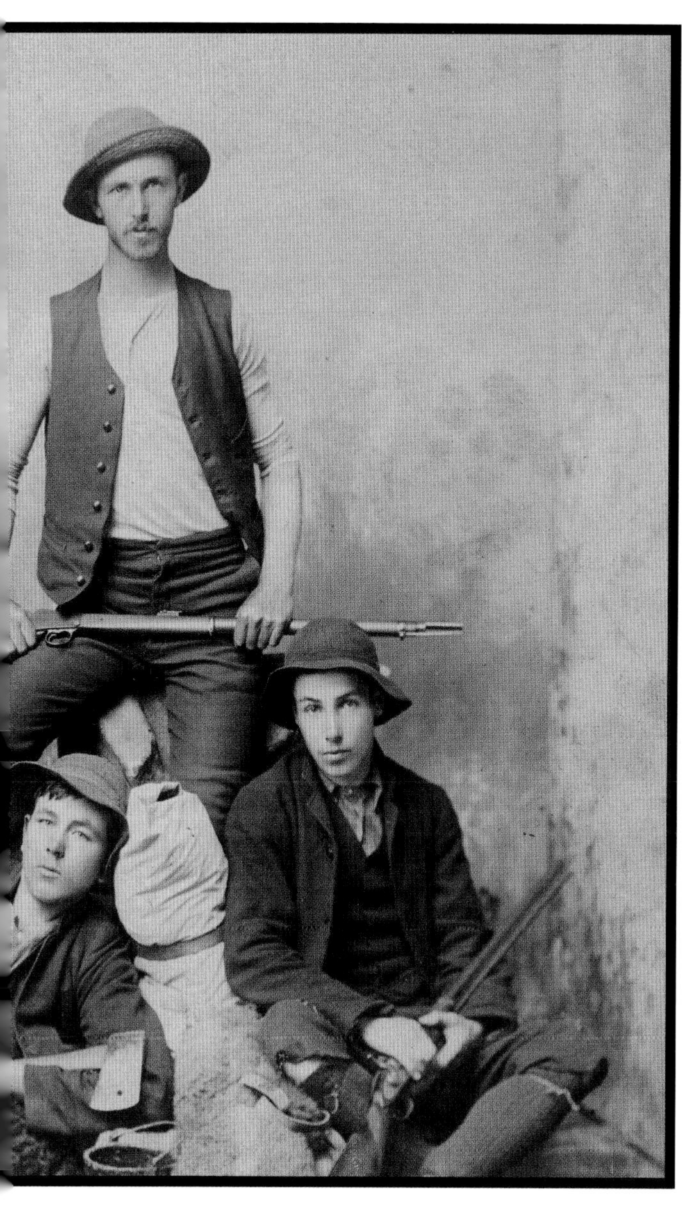

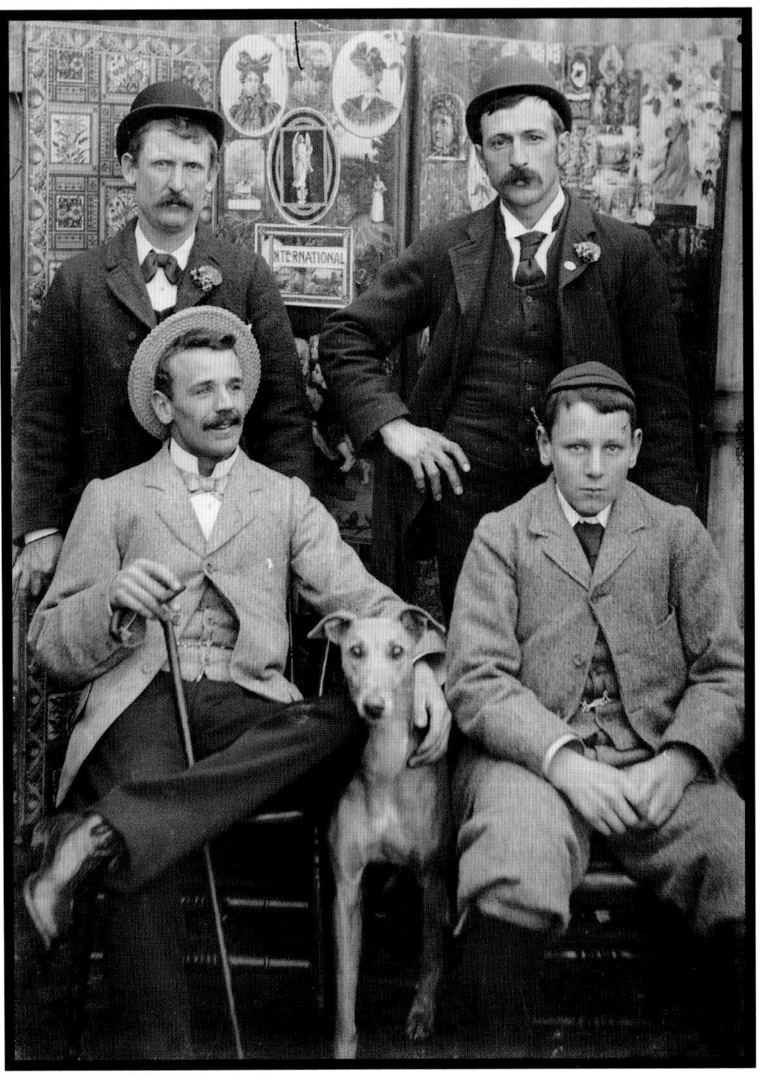
INTERNATIONAL

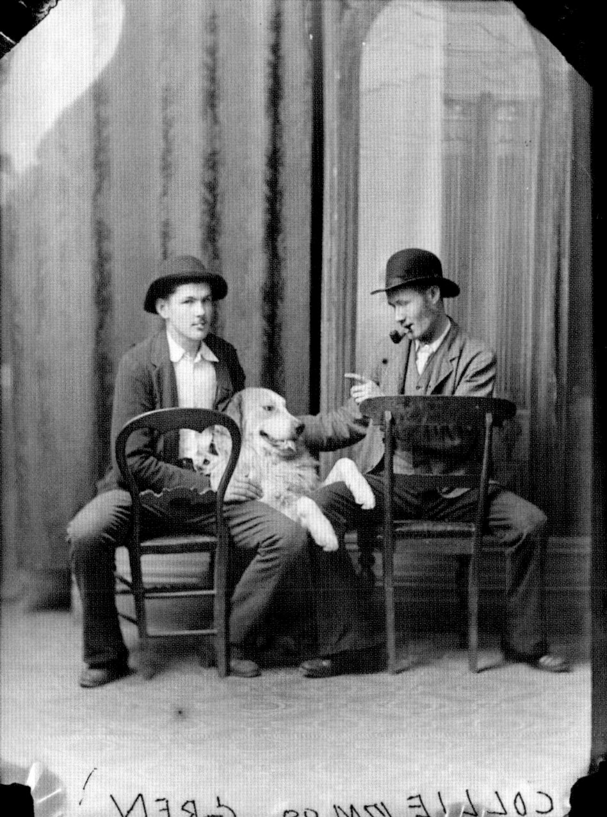

The tennis star's dog

Carlo, who was possibly a Springer spaniel, was the family pet of the well-connected Wilding family of Christchurch. Beside him in this photograph taken around 1889 is five-year-old Anthony Wilding (1883–1915), who went on to become arguably the first global superstar of tennis before being killed in action during the First World War.

Anthony started playing tennis when he was six, on two courts (grass and asphalt) at the family's property in the Heathcote Valley. It's likely that Carlo would have had plenty of balls to chase before Anthony left home to attend school and university in England.

Wilding dominated international tennis, winning eleven Grand Slams, four Davis Cups (representing Australasia) and a bronze medal at the 1912 Olympic Games. He still holds several all-time singles tennis records, and is, to date, the only player from New Zealand to have won a Grand Slam singles title. Wilding was also a keen and accomplished cricketer, rugby player and motorcyclist, frequently motorcycling to tennis tournaments on the European continent.

At the outbreak of war, Wilding, who was in Britain, first joined the Royal Marines and was subsequently the captain of an armoured car squadron in northern France. He was killed during the Battle of Aubers Ridge in May 1915, aged thirty-one. The Christchurch tennis centre Wilding Park is named after him.

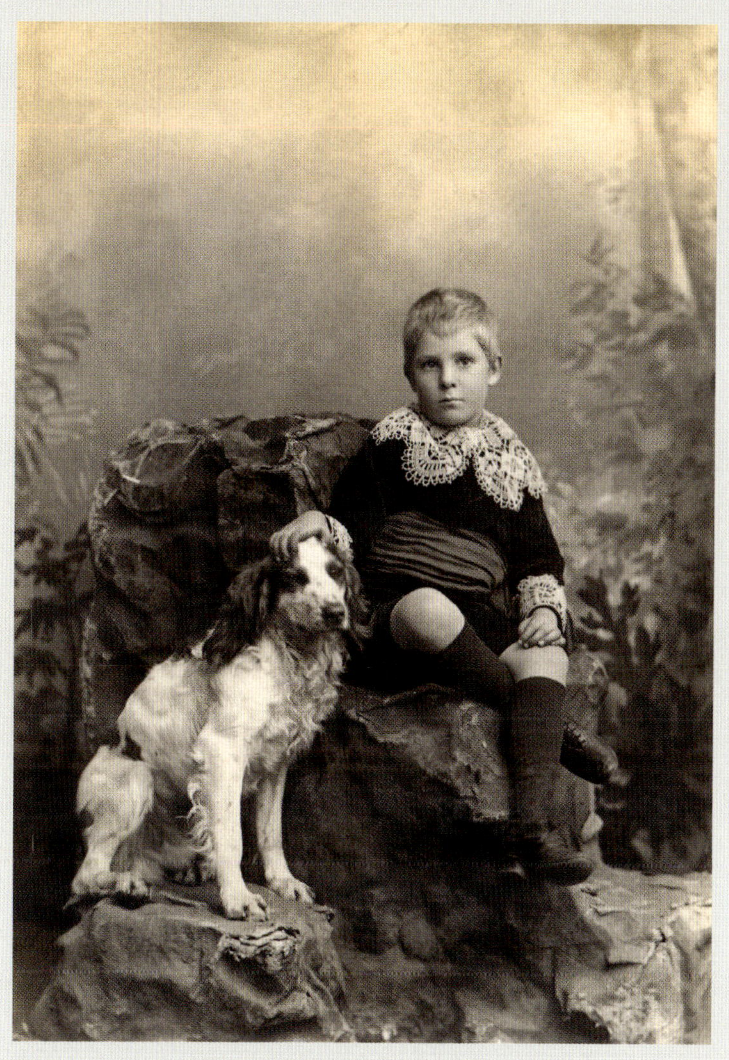

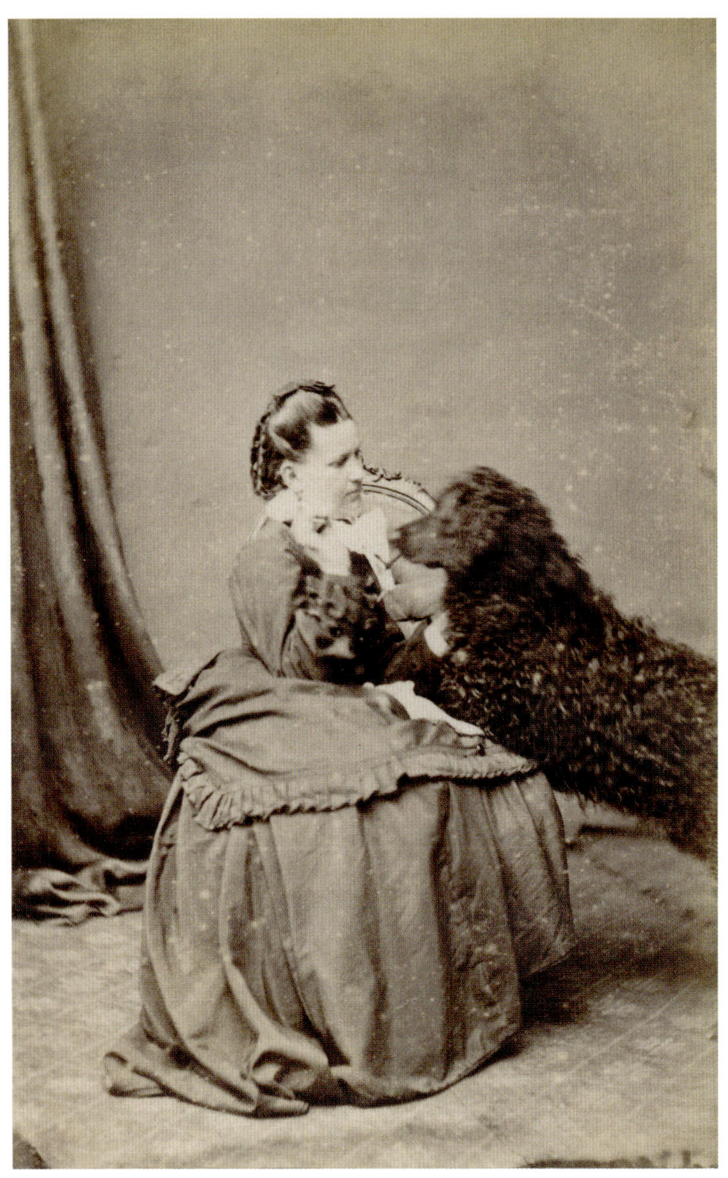

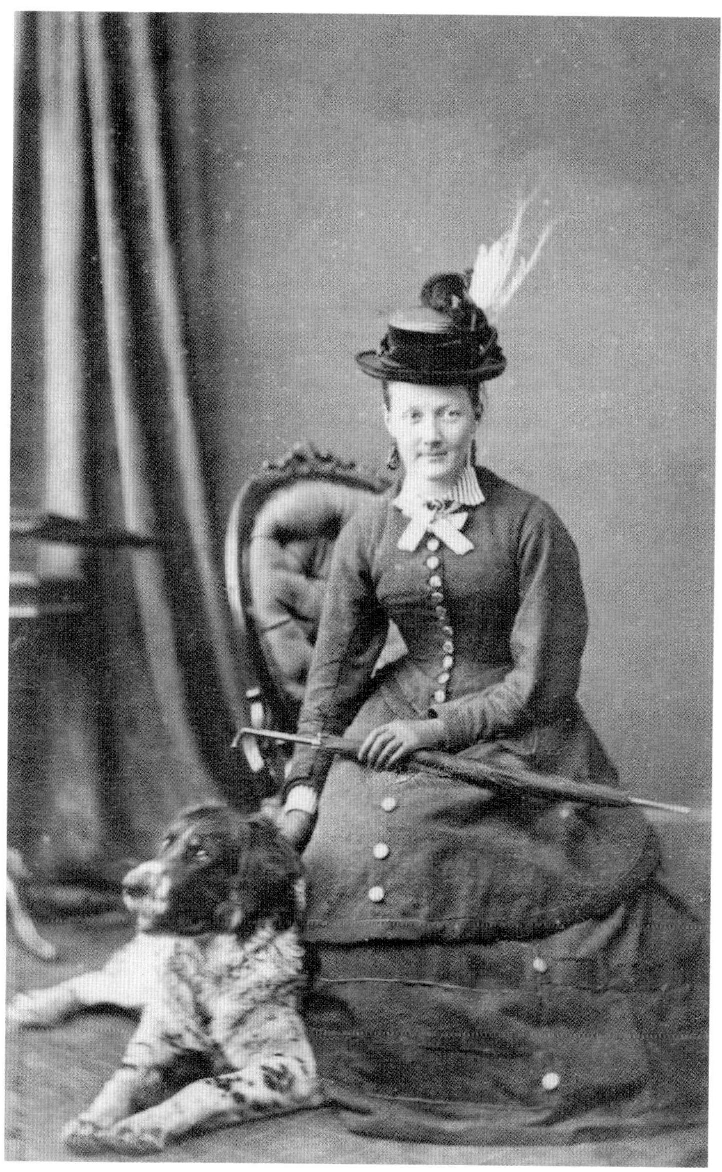

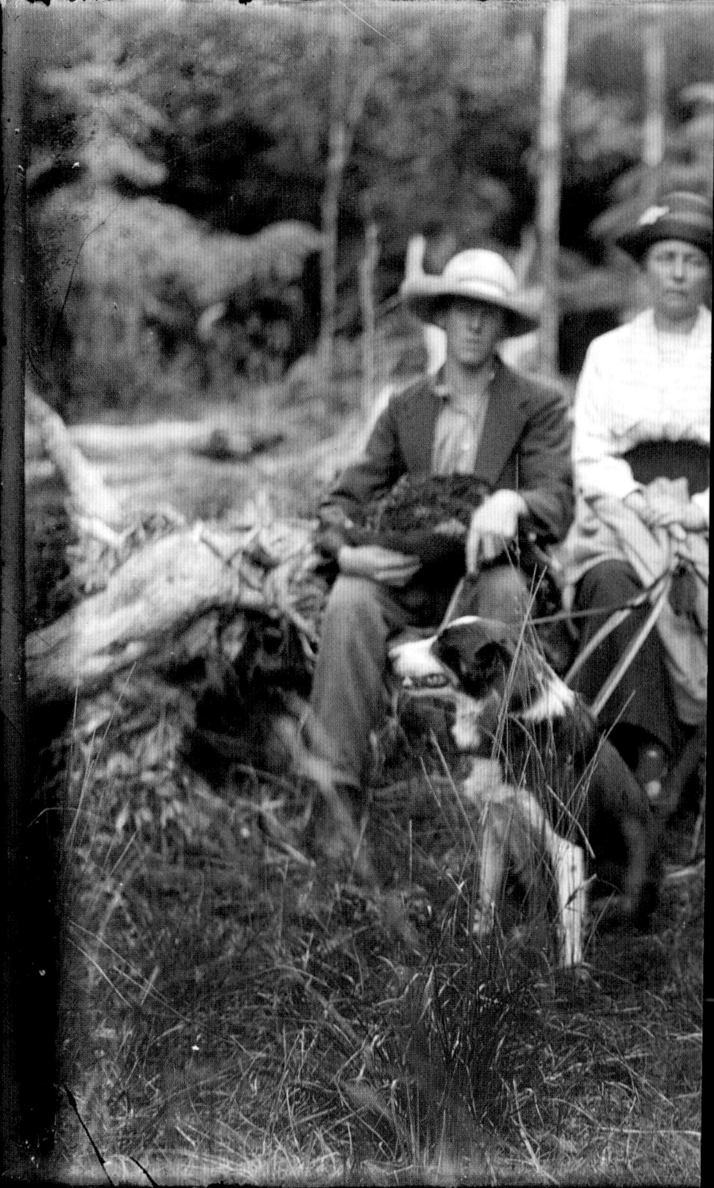

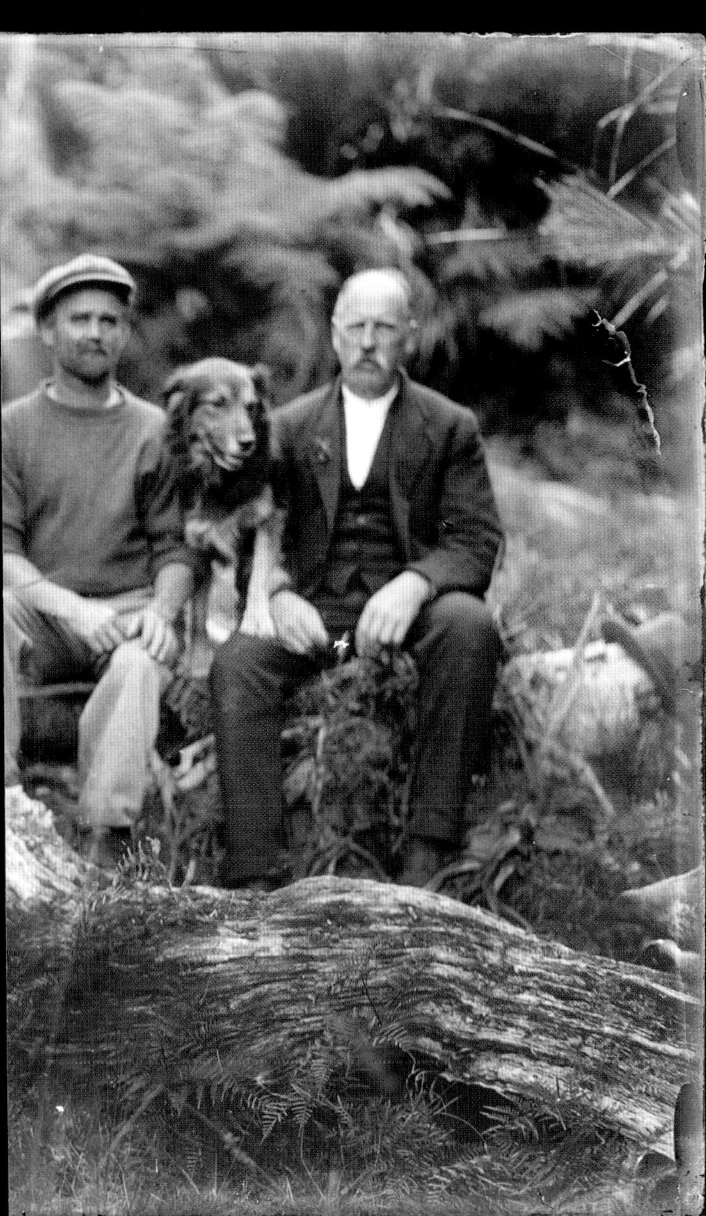

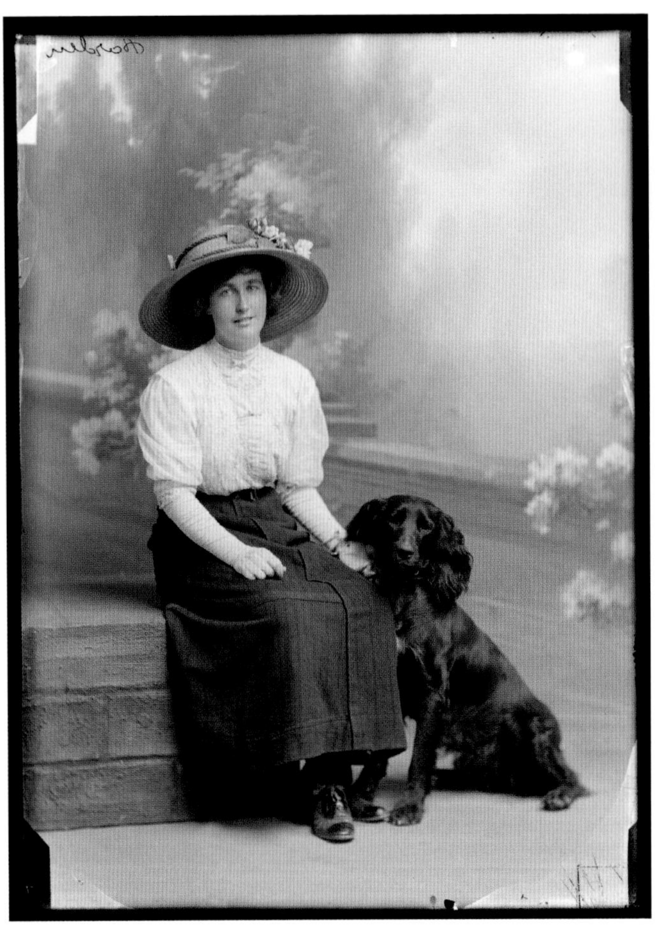

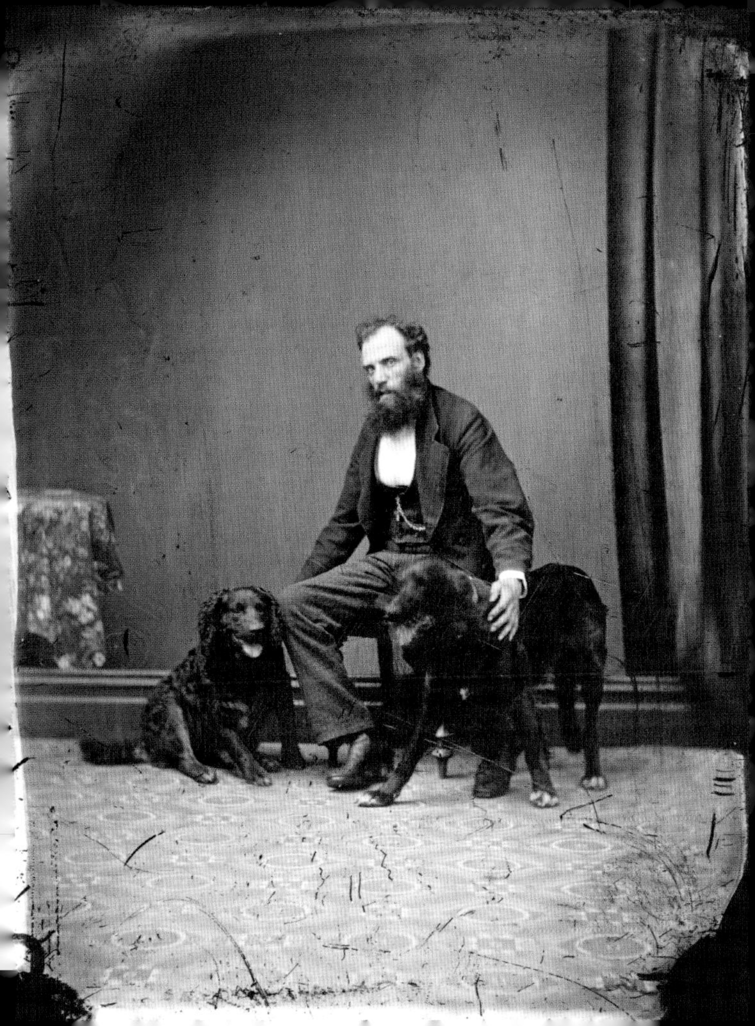

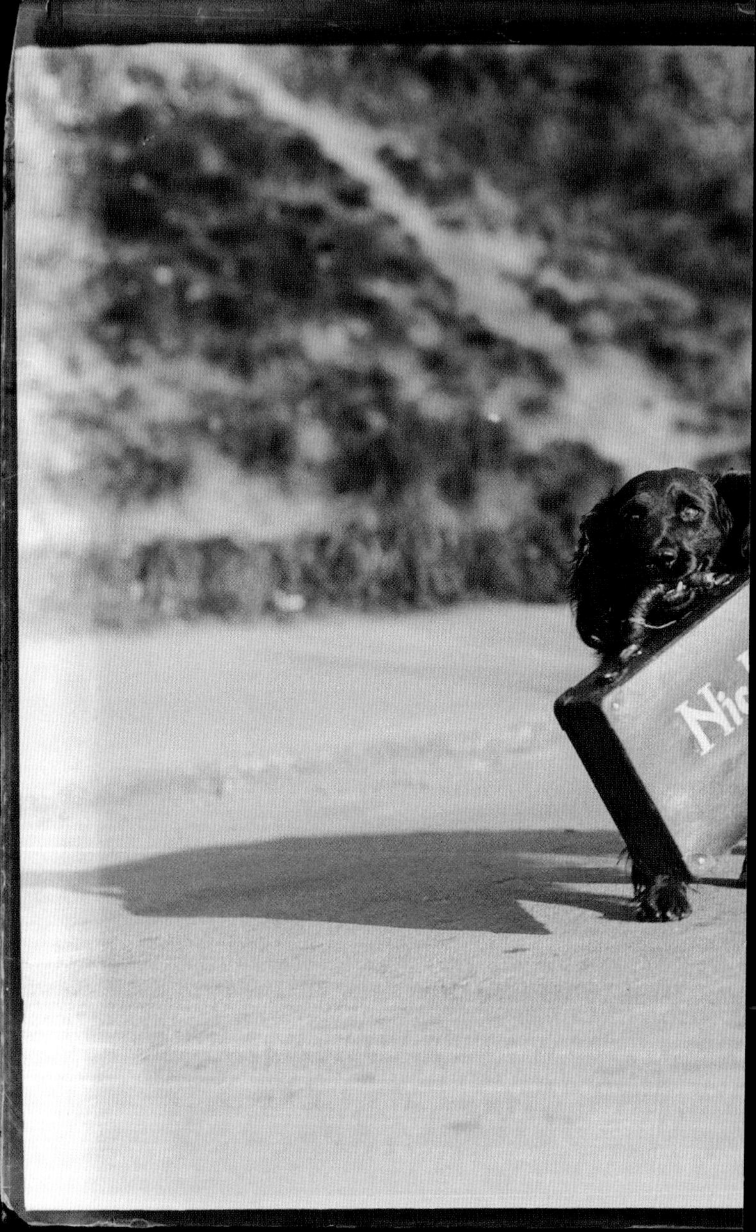

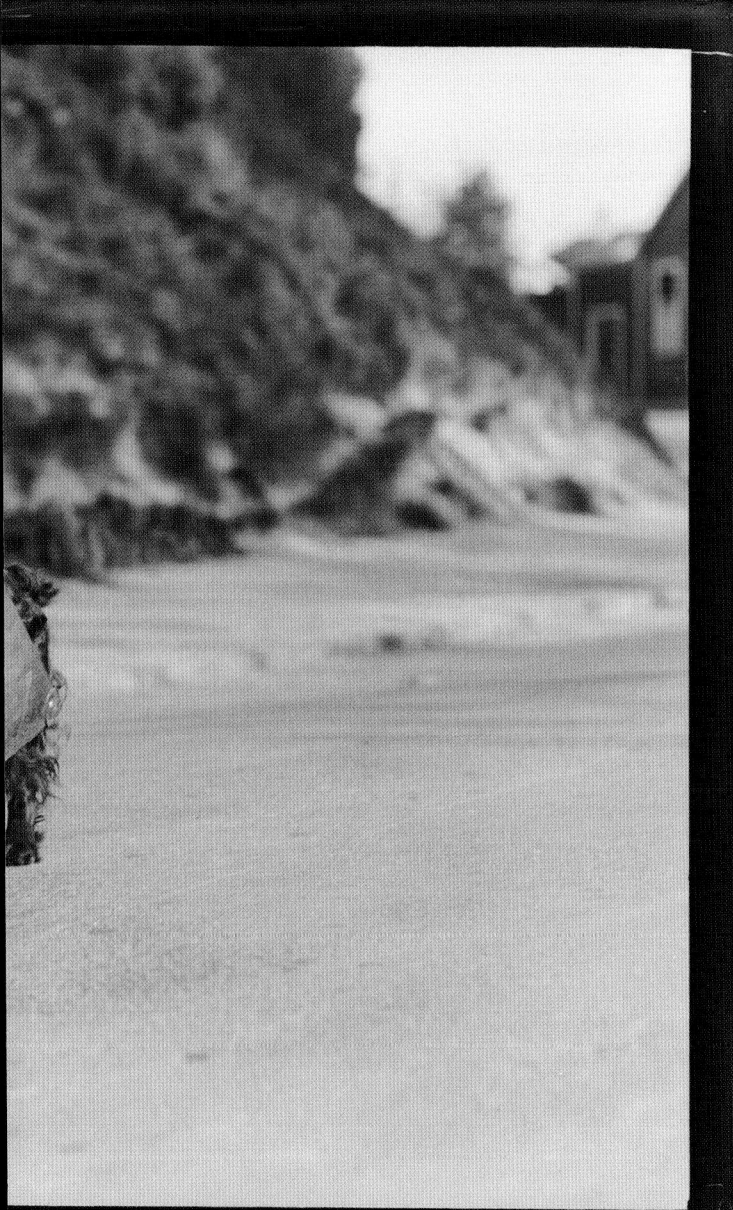

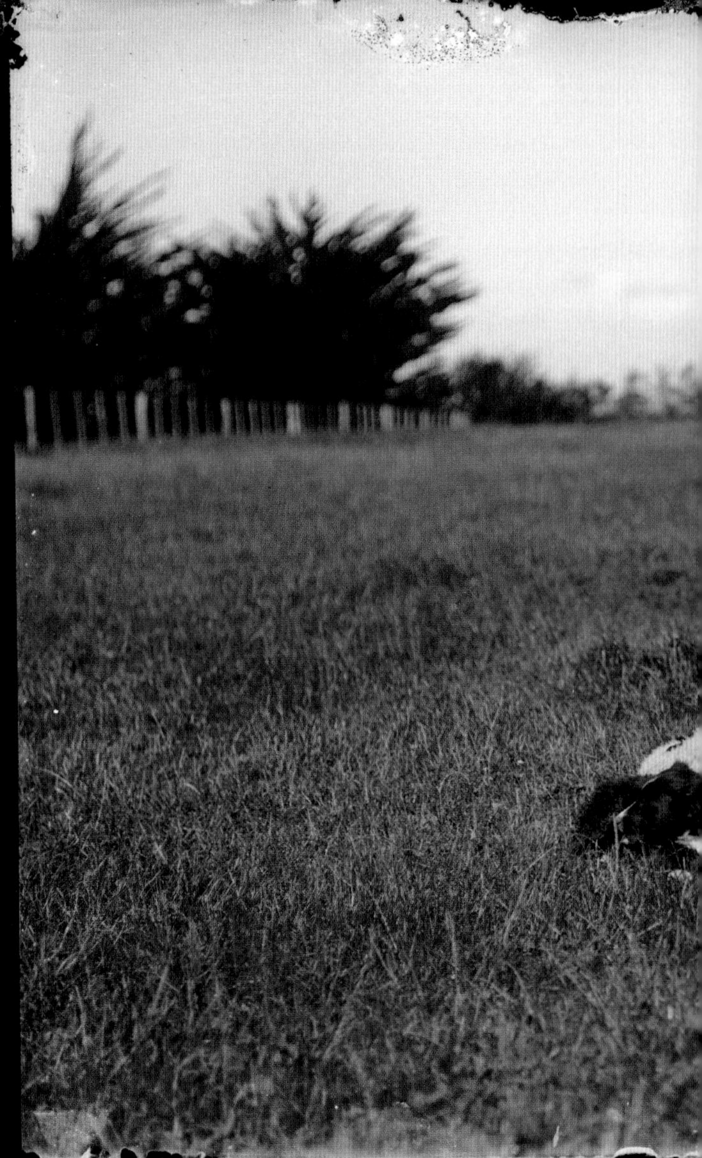

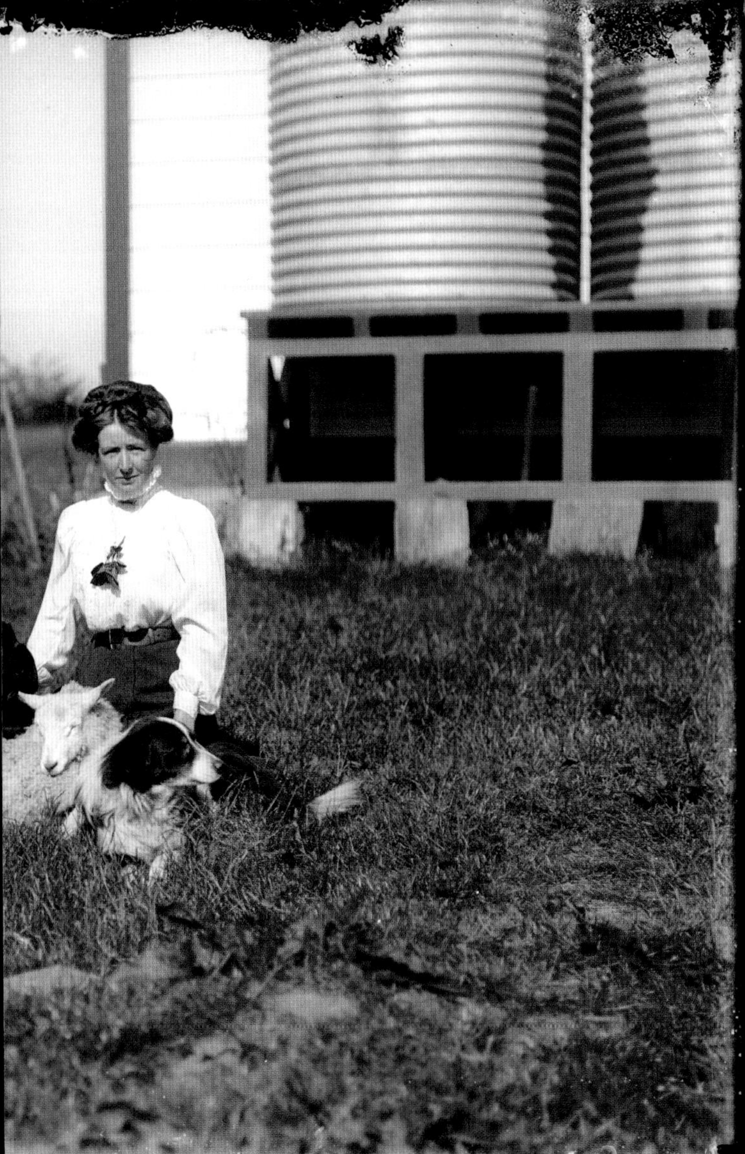

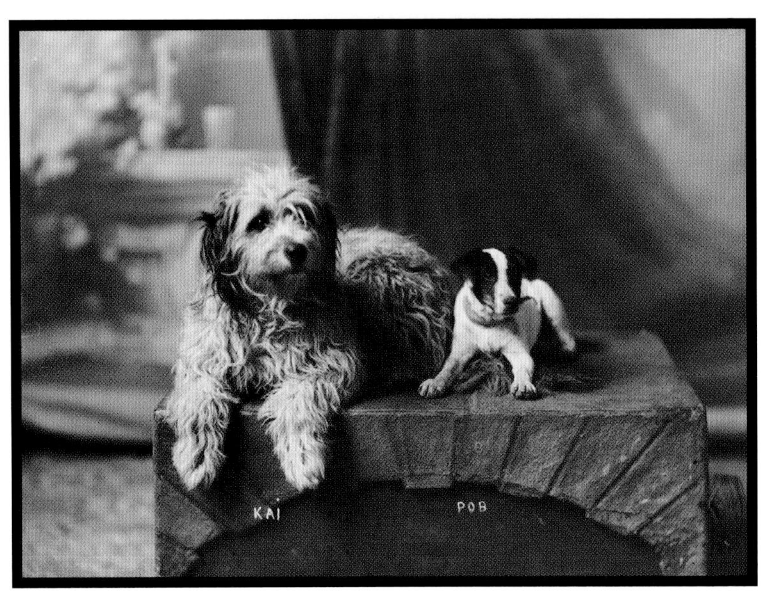
KAI
POB

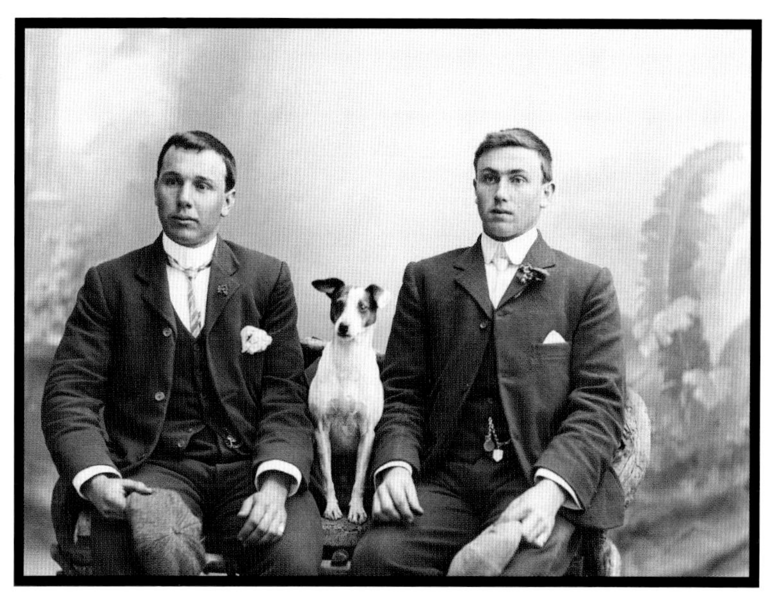

The sled dog

The impressive and apparently charismatic husky known as Osman was recruited from Siberia with thirty other experienced sledding dogs for Robert Falcon Scott's 1910 expedition to Antarctica. He was shipped to New Zealand, where he and the rest of the pack trained on Quail Island in Lyttelton Harbour, pulling wheeled sleds over dirt tracks (see page 30).

Scott's ship *Terra Nova* left Lyttelton for Antarctica on 29 November 1910, and Osman and the other dogs endured a miserable time chained to the deck throughout the journey south. During one storm Osman's chain broke and he was swept overboard, only to be tossed back on deck by a subsequent wave. Life on the ice was no less perilous, and he dodged death when a sledging party fell into a crevasse. Little wonder Scott thought Osman was his best sled dog.

The *Terra Nova* returned to New Zealand in 1913 without Scott, Edgar Evans, Titus Oates, Henry Bowers and Edward Wilson, who had all died returning from the South Pole, but with Osman and many of the other dogs. Osman initially lived near Christchurch with his Russian dog-handler, but by 1916 he was one of the most famous residents of the Wellington Zoo, where he was joined a year later by some of the dogs from Shackleton's Imperial Trans-Antarctic Expedition supply ship *Aurora*. It is thought that he died in 1918, aged ten. Canterbury Museum holds his collar.

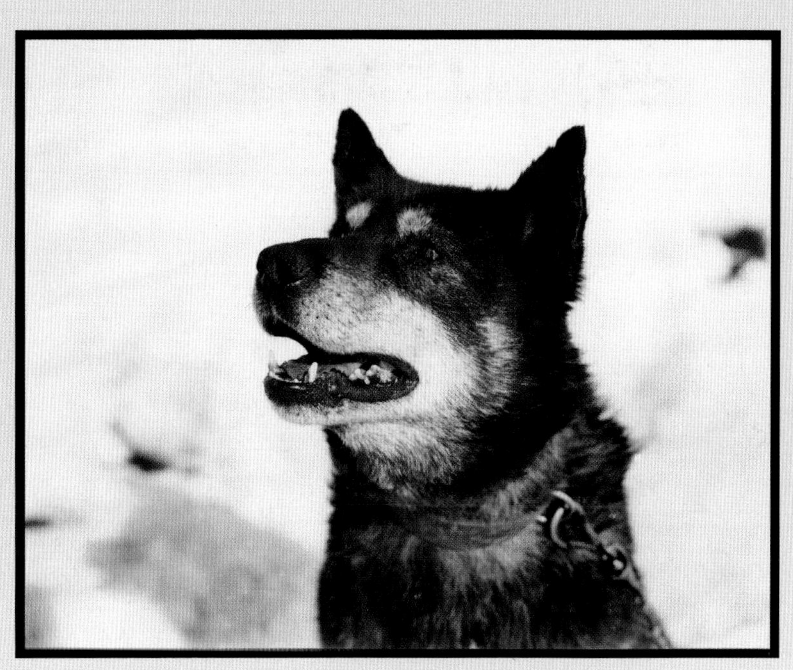

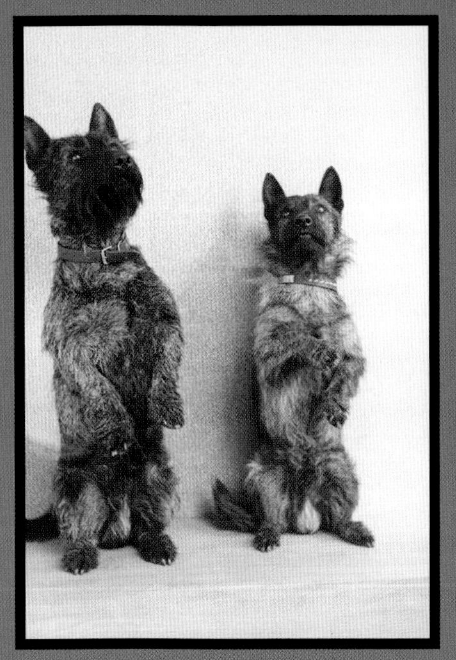

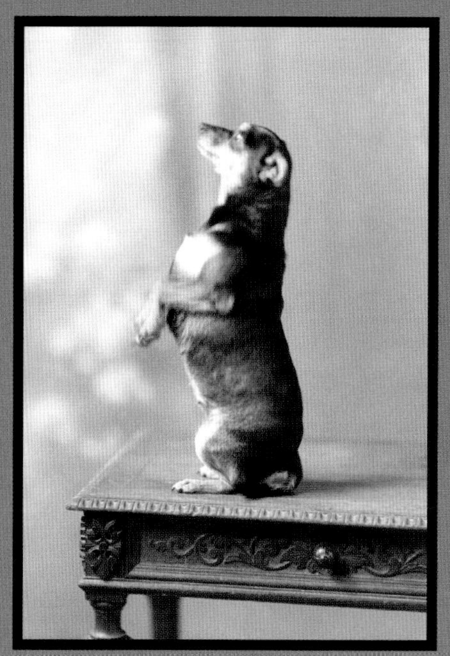

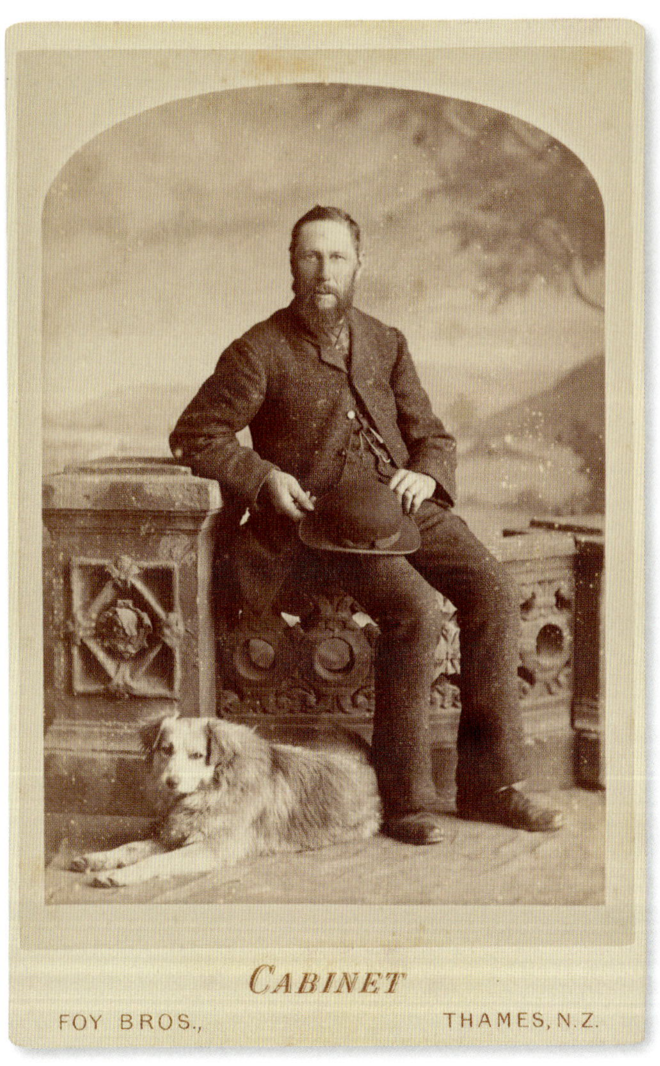
CABINET
FOY BROS.,
THAMES, N.Z.

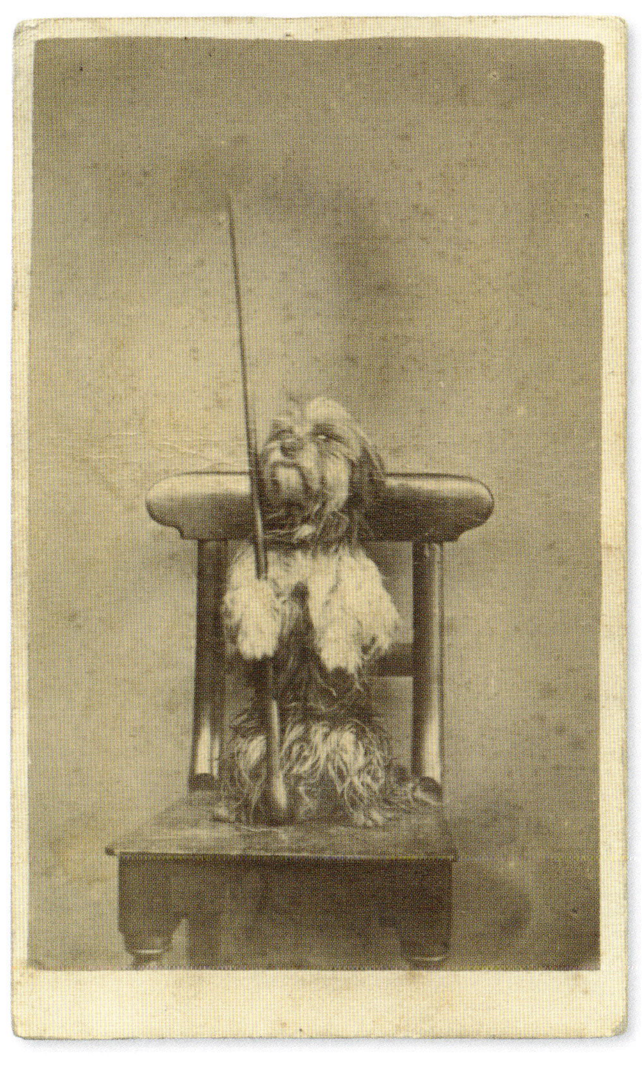

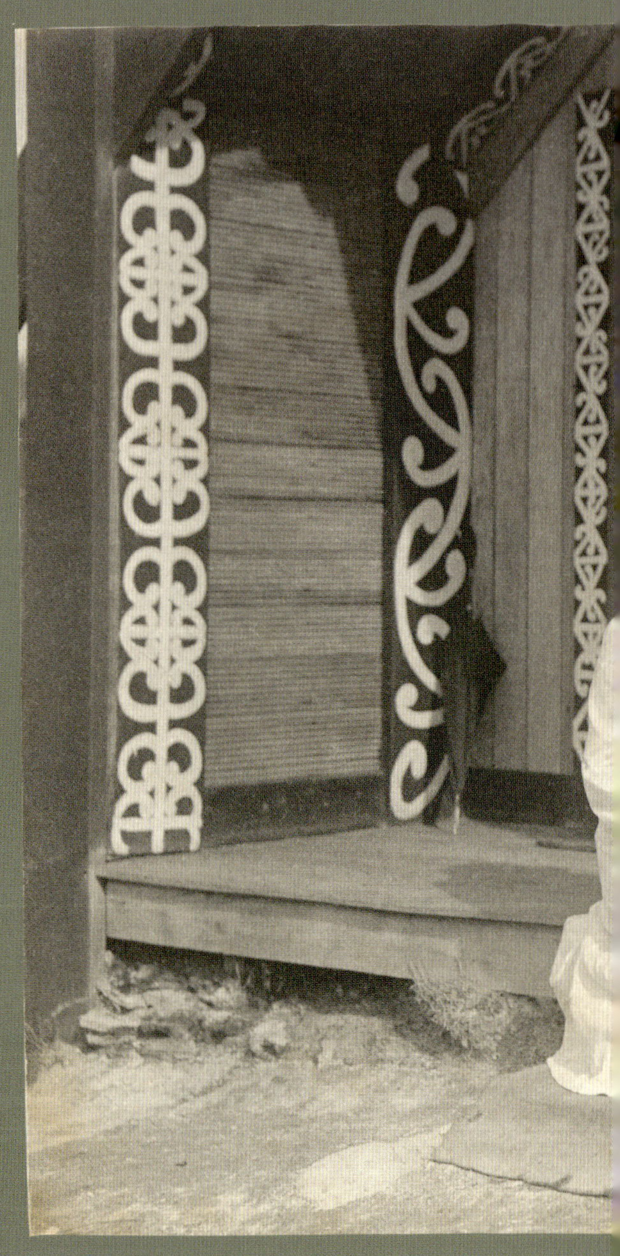

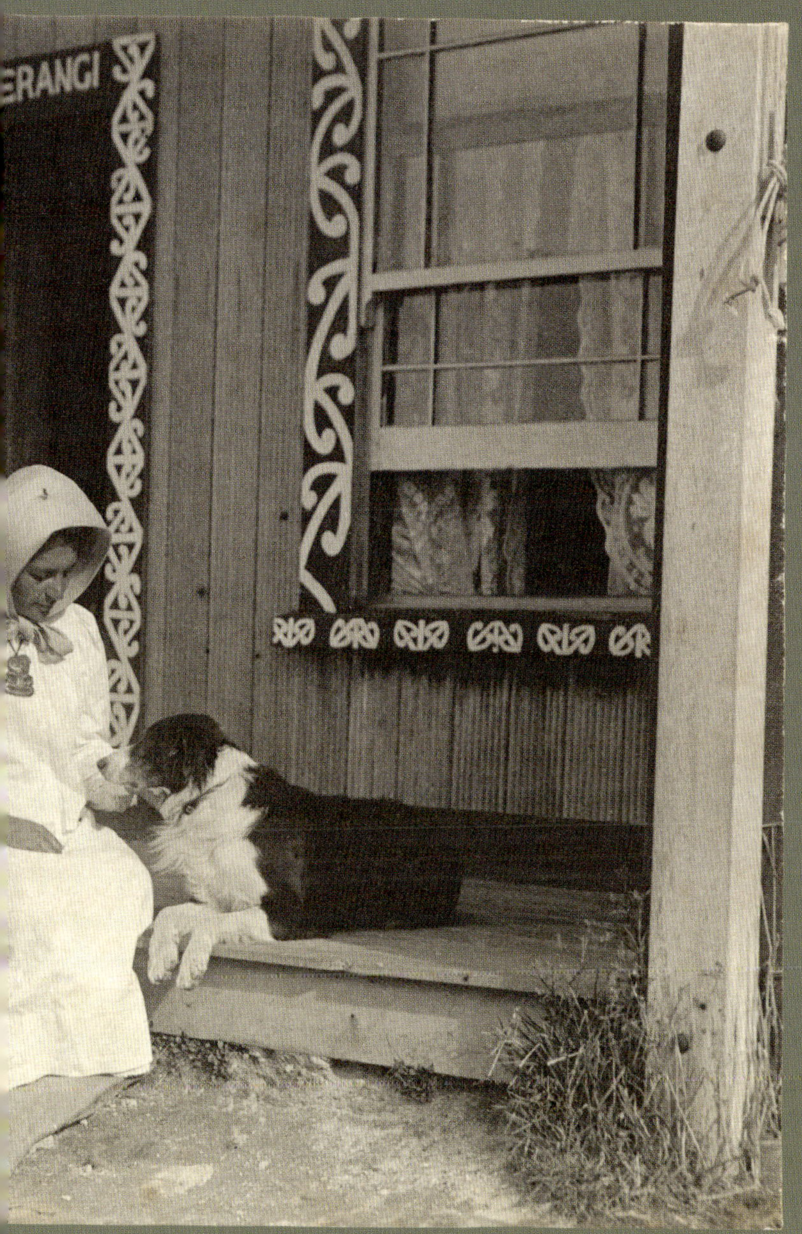
ERANGI

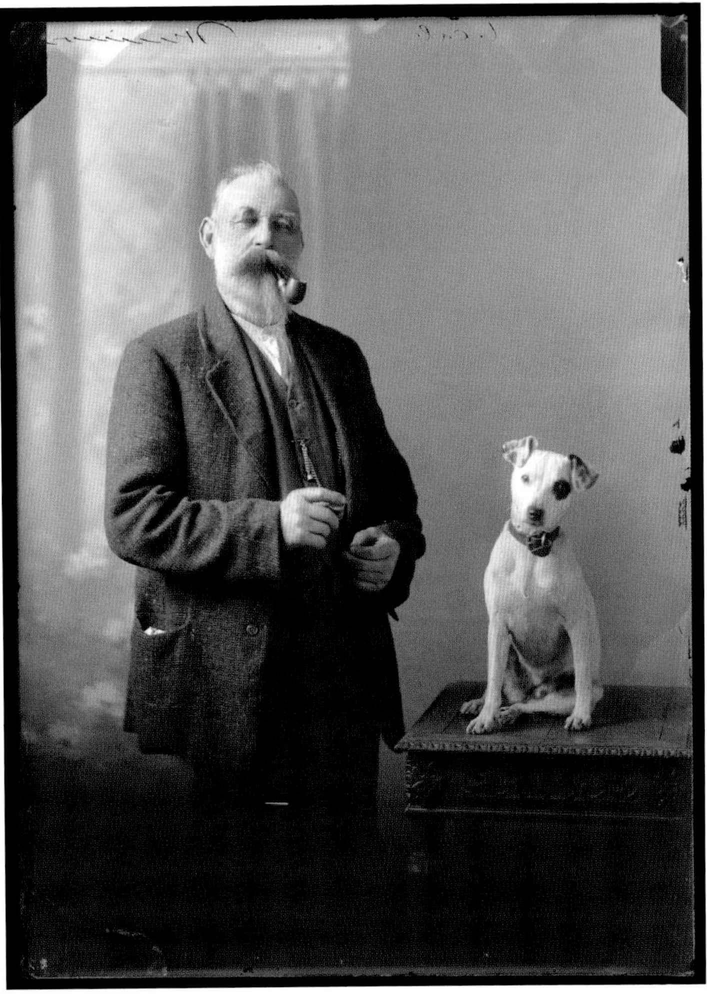

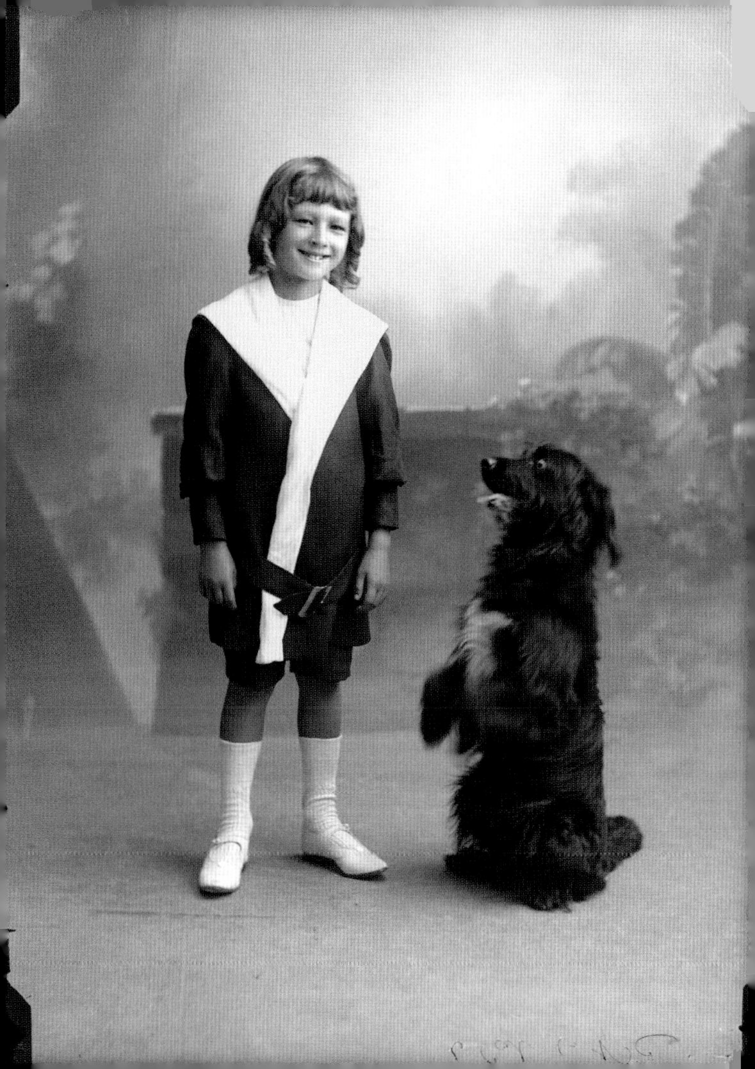

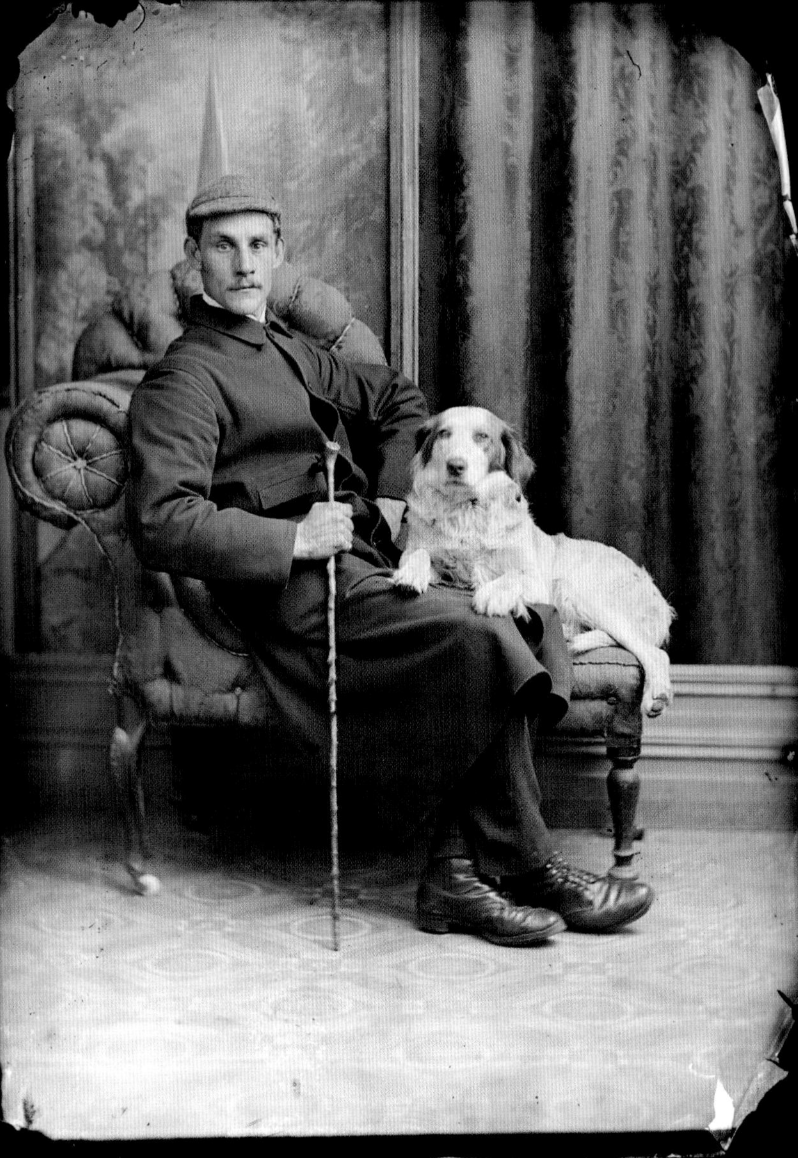

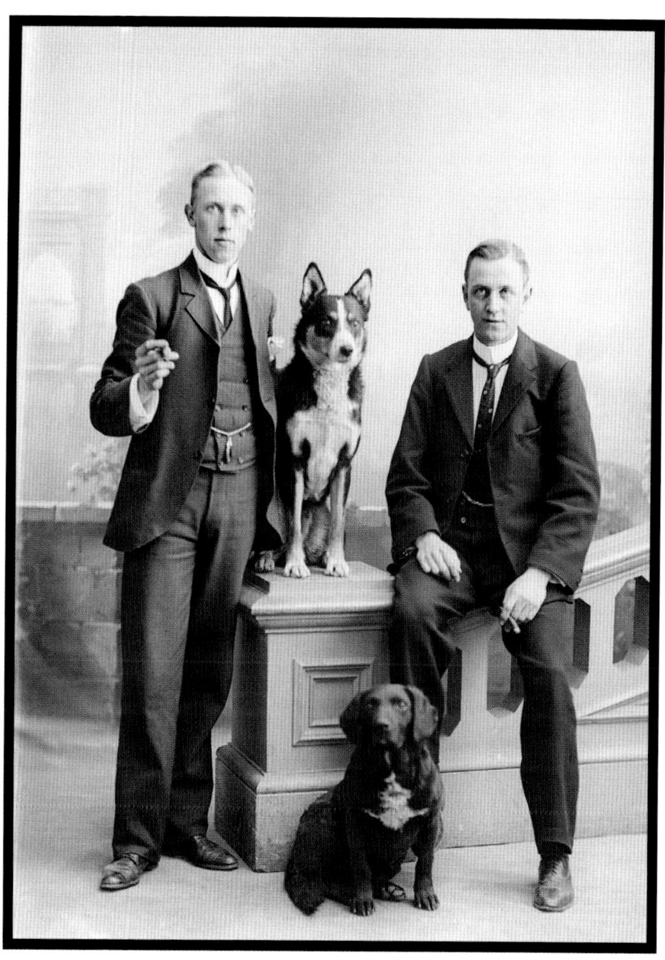

The photographer: Tyree studio

Tyree studio was founded by William Tyree (1855–1924) in 1882 in Trafalgar Street, Nelson, several years after he arrived from England with his family. Tyree specialised in studio portraits, exterior views and civic occasions of the Nelson region. William's younger brother, Fred (see page 104), worked for him briefly before establishing his own photographic business in Tākaka in 1889.

Rose Frank started working at the Tyree studio in 1886 and was responsible for the studio portraits. When William Tyree left for Australia in 1895, he appointed her as manager of the studio. Having run the business for fifteen years, she finally bought it in 1914. Frank retired in 1950, after sixty-one years as a photographer.

The Tyree studio collection of over 100,000 surviving glass-plate negatives was donated by Rose Frank to the Nelson Historical Society in the 1950s. It is a treasure trove of early portraiture. UNESCO's Memory of the World Trust included the collection on New Zealand's documentary heritage register in 2017.

Some images list the names of the subjects, but the museum did not always inherit information other than surnames and catalogue numbers. In the case of this image, the title is simply 'Jones'. Nelson Provincial Museum encourages the public to add information or stories via the museum's online collections.

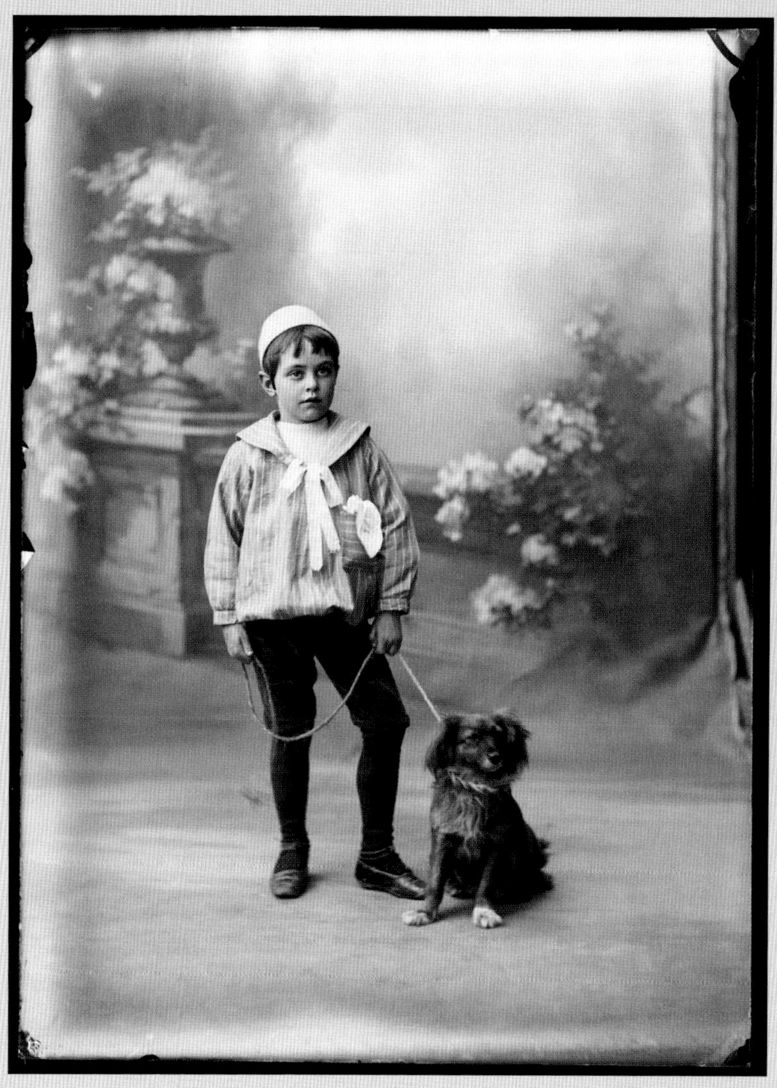

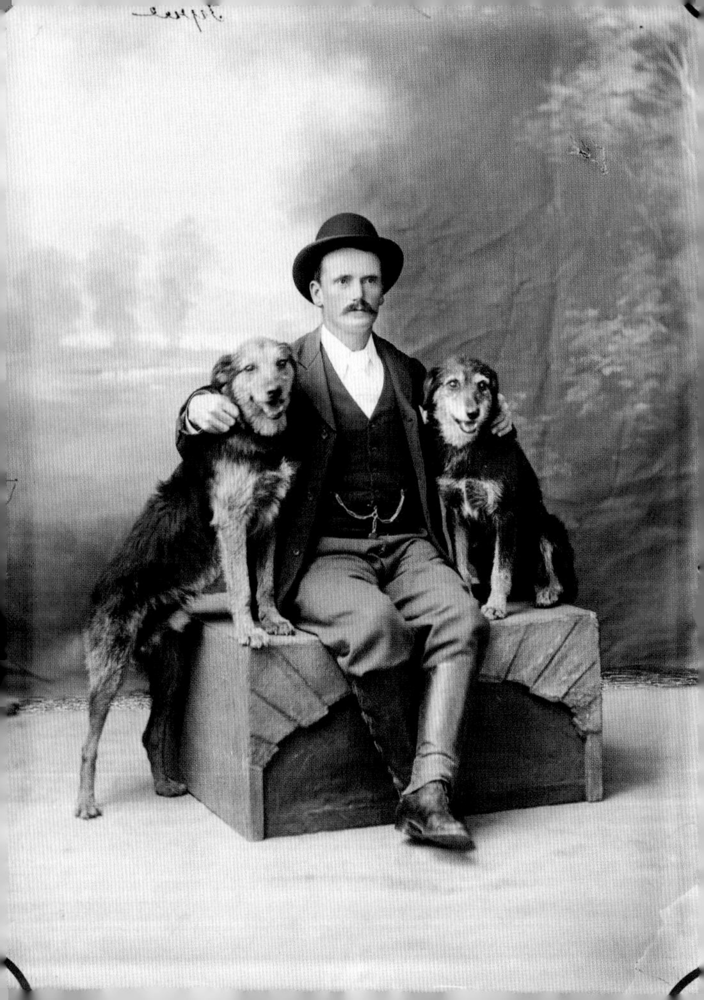

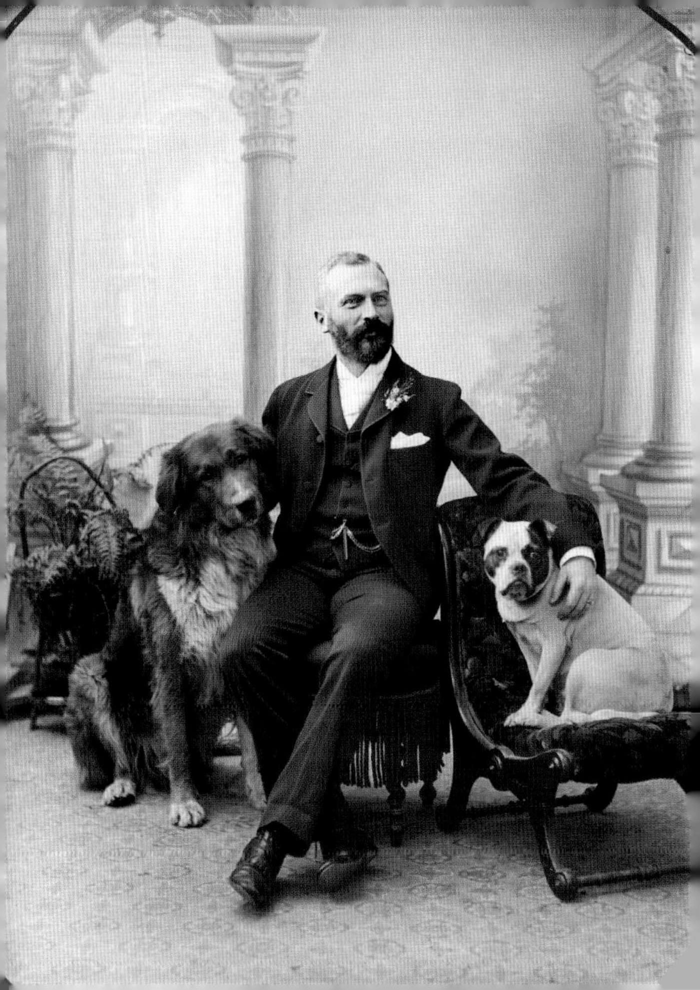

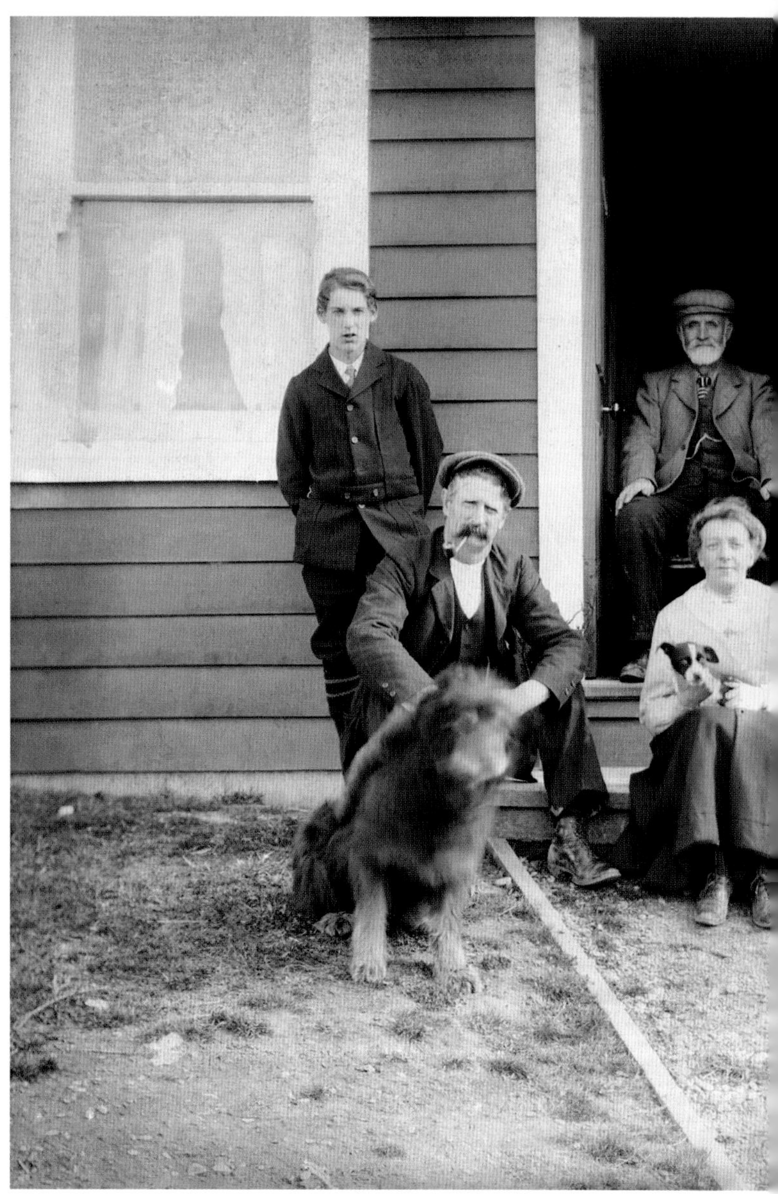

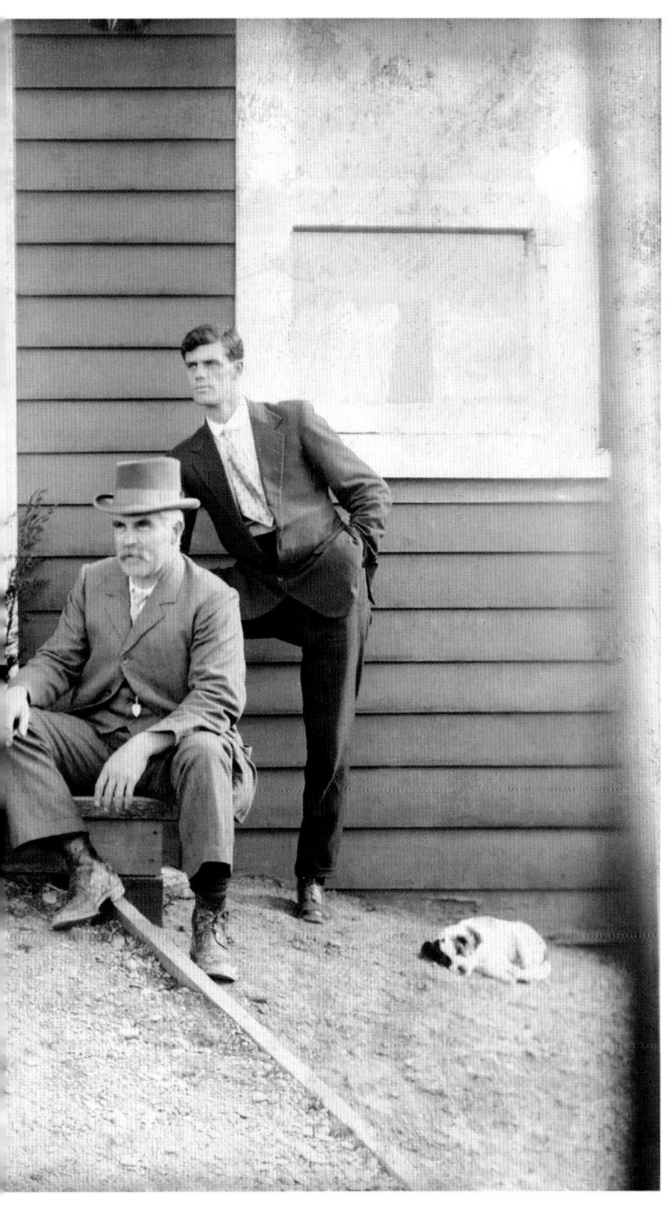

The photographer: William J Harding

William James Harding (1826–1899) and his wife, Annie, arrived in New Zealand from London in 1855. In England, Harding had been a coach builder, and initially he turned his hand to cabinet-making when the couple settled in Whanganui, before establishing a photographic studio on Ridgway Street in the 1860s. Competition among Whanganui photographers at the time was fierce, and, although Harding preferred landscape work, portraiture offered better financial security. *The Wanganui Herald* remarked that Harding seemed to prefer making beautiful art to making money, and that his studio was not as elaborately fitted out as those of his rivals. Despite this he created striking images, including this portrait of 'Mr Frank and his acrobatic dog'.

The studio struggled financially into the 1880s. William and Annie eventually moved to Sydney to live with their daughter, leaving behind more than 6000 negatives showing settlers and landscapes in the Manawatū and Rangitīkei areas – a significant record of the colonial experience.

Large quantities of glass-plate negatives were produced in New Zealand from the 1850s. However, they were bulky and heavy, and many have been lost or broken. The Alexander Turnbull Library acquired most of Harding's negatives as part of a major acquisition campaign from the late 1940s. In recent decades, digitisation of glass-plate negative collections has brought thousands of previously unseen images of ordinary New Zealanders to light. Other images from this collection are on pages 15, 16, 75, 83, 100 and 131.

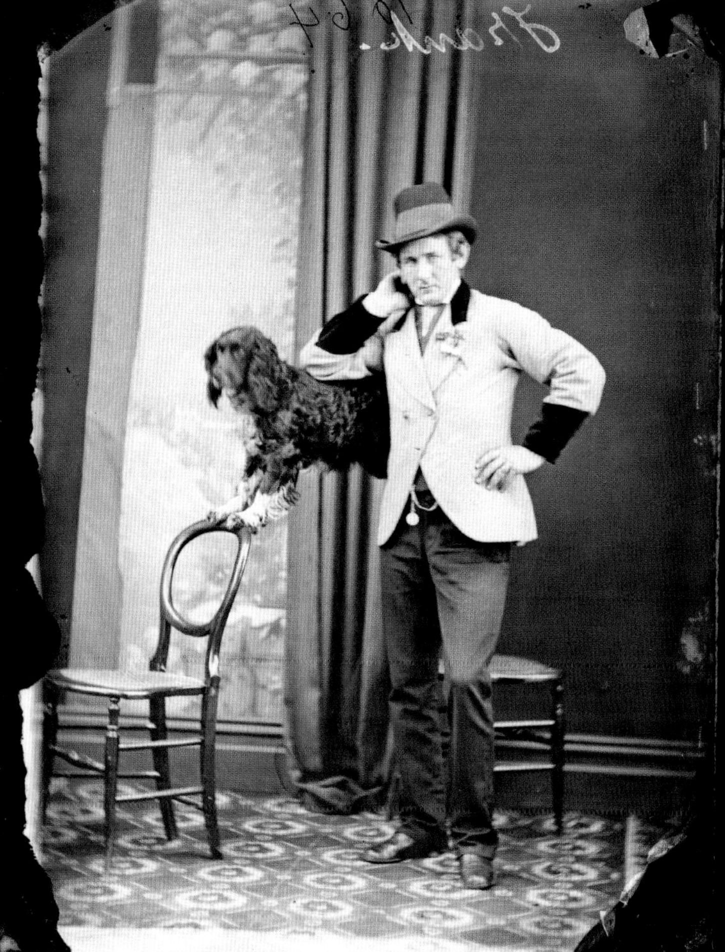

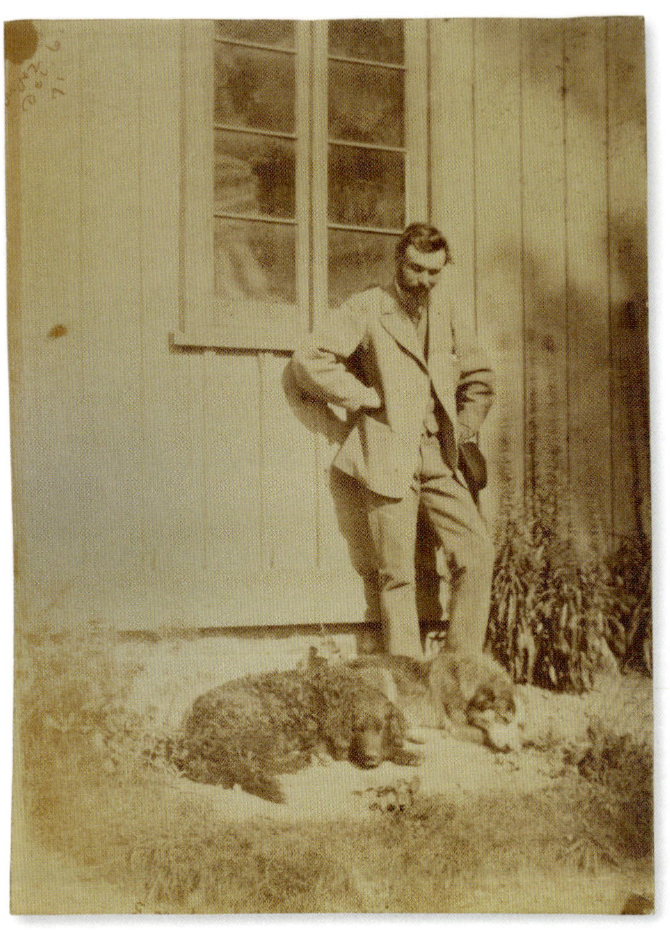

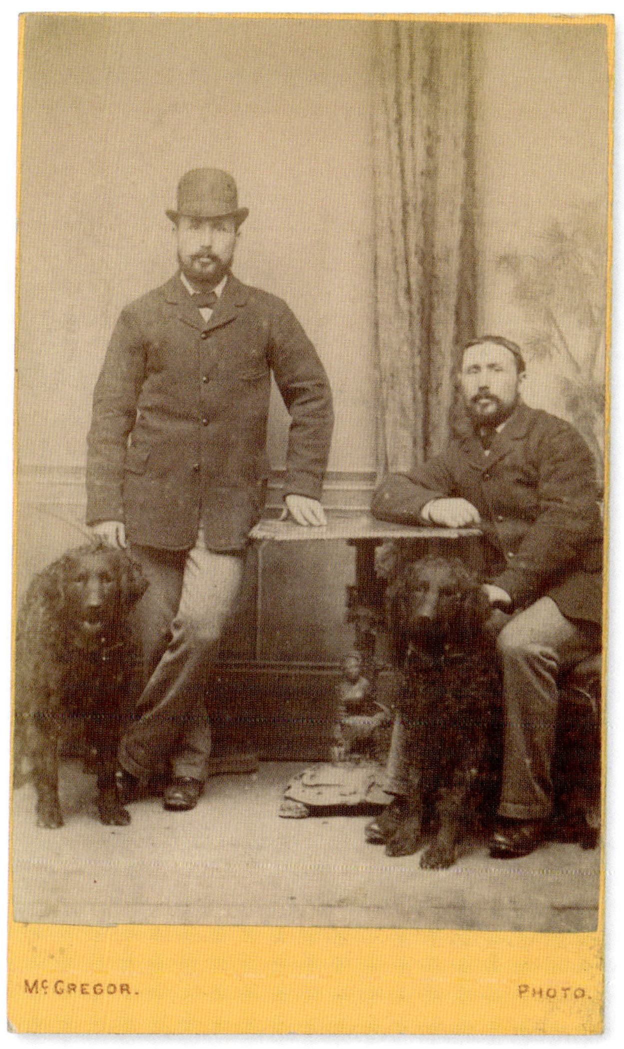
Mc GREGOR.
PHOTO.

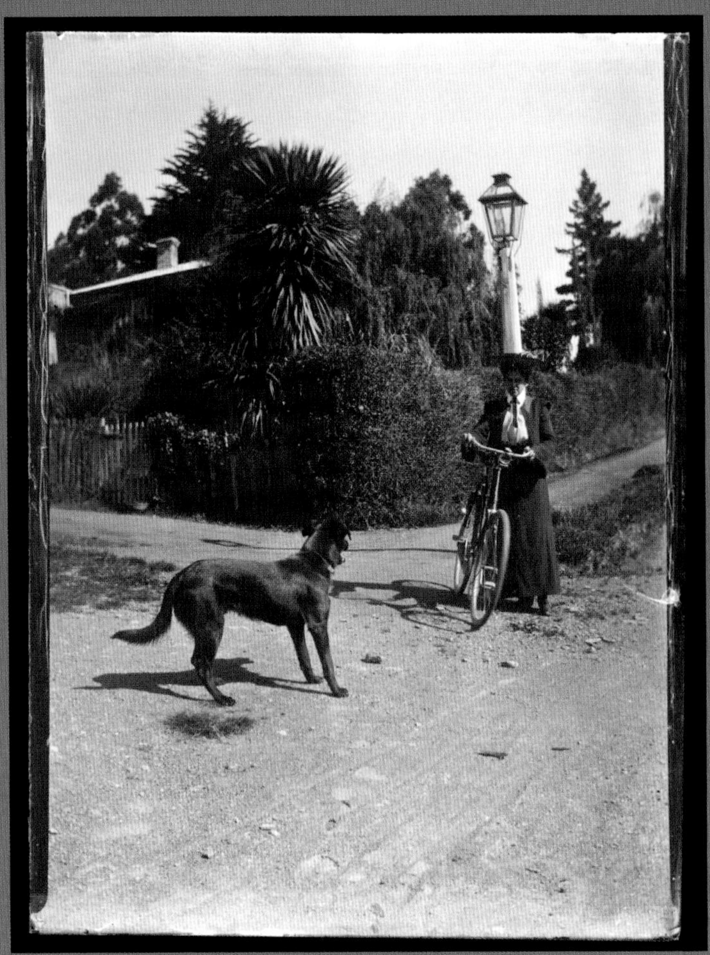

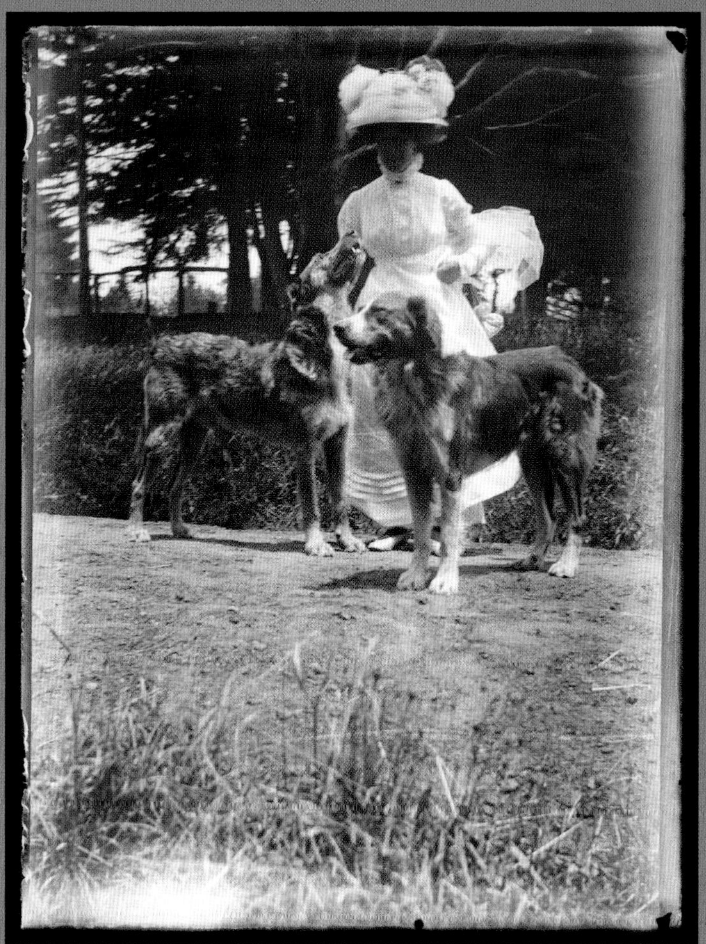

The miners' dog

This photograph of coal miners and three dogs (one appears blurred alongside the man sitting to the right) was taken by a Tyree studio photographer at Pākawau in Golden Bay some time in the late 1890s or early 1900s. The miners are, from left: unknown, Charlie Crook, Jim Walker (mine manager from 1896), unknown, Frank Flowers, Charlie Curnow, [first name unknown] King, Fred Field and Jack Shaw. Coal mining began at the small Pākawau mine after the gold ran out in the area in the 1860s. By the 1890s, coal mining was a sizeable business in the Collingwood area, with first a deep-water wharf being built and then a railway line that linked the mines to the coal port at Pūponga. However, difficulties set in, and not long after the First World War mining had ceased in the district.

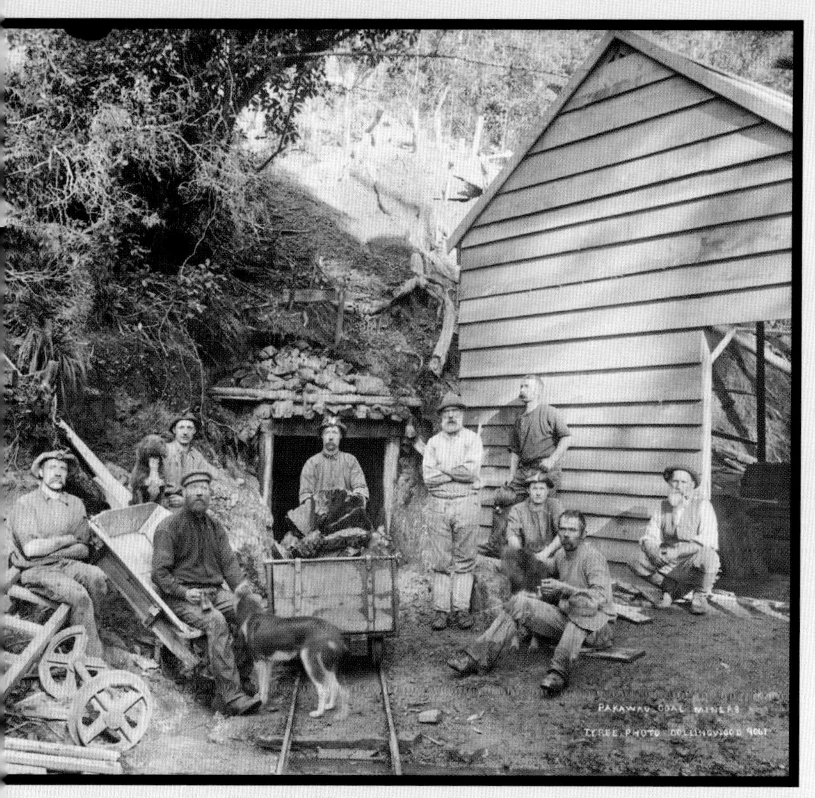
PAKAWAU COAL MINERS

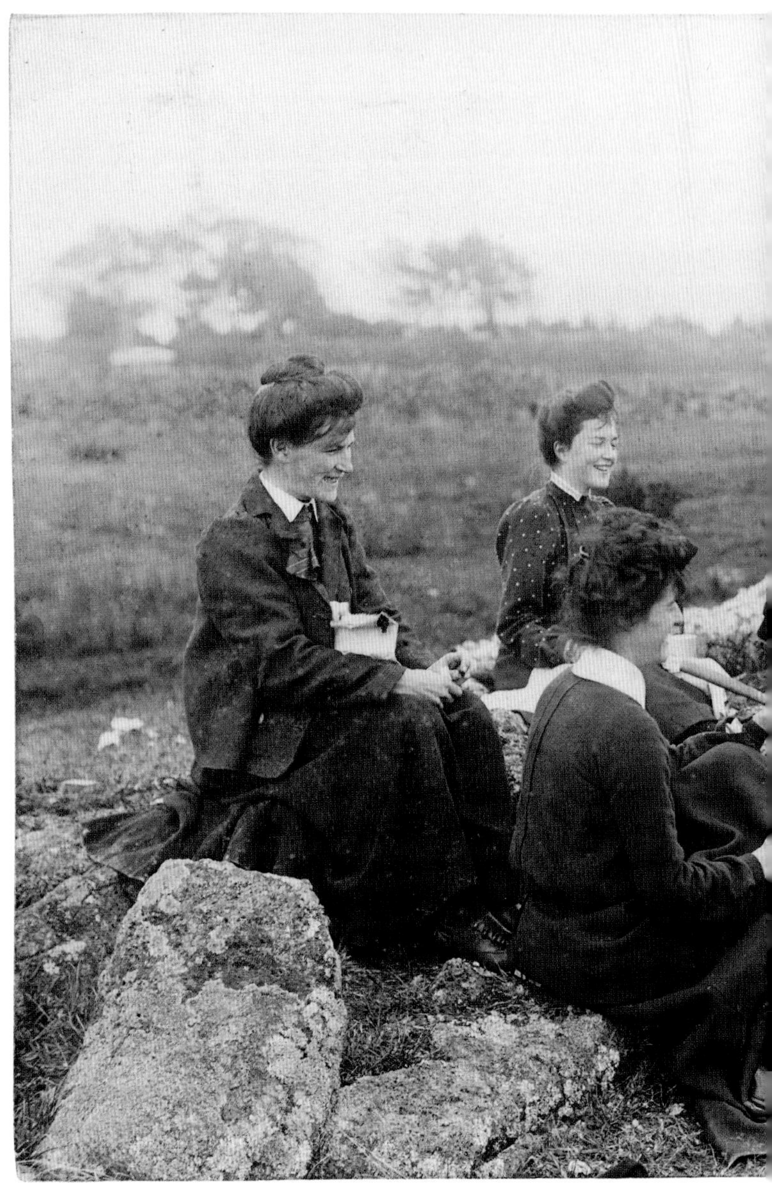

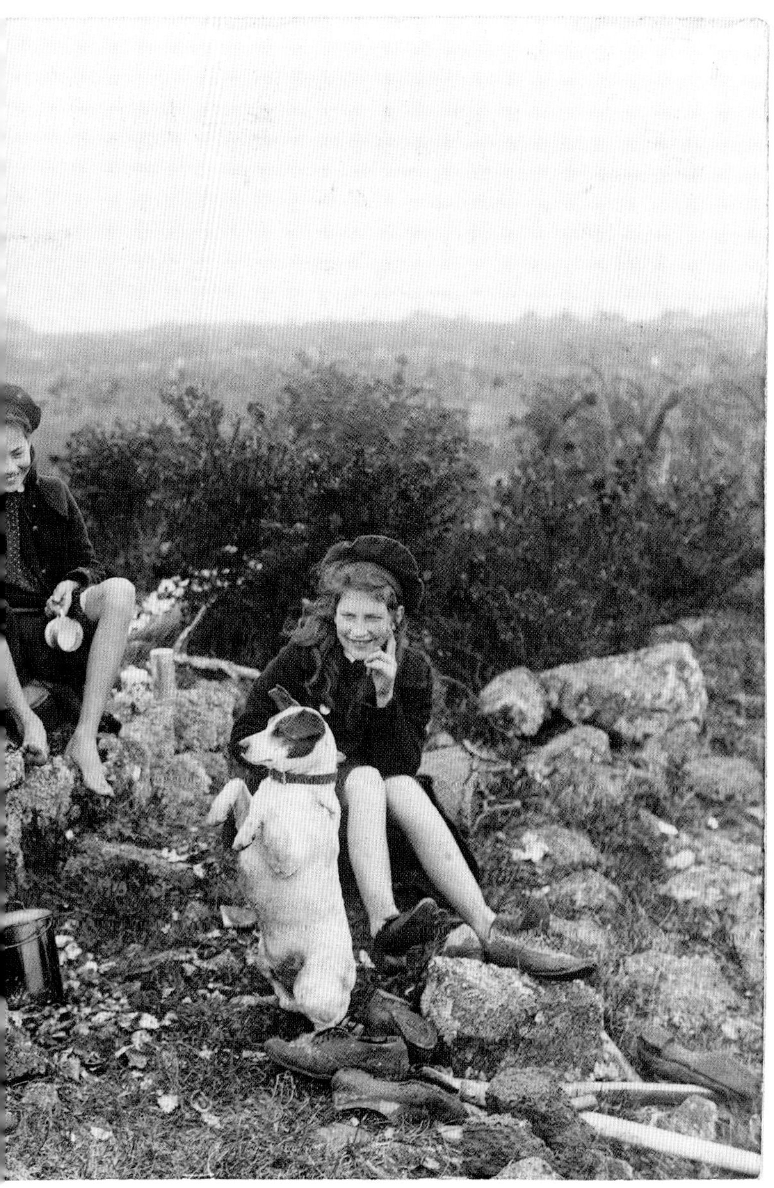

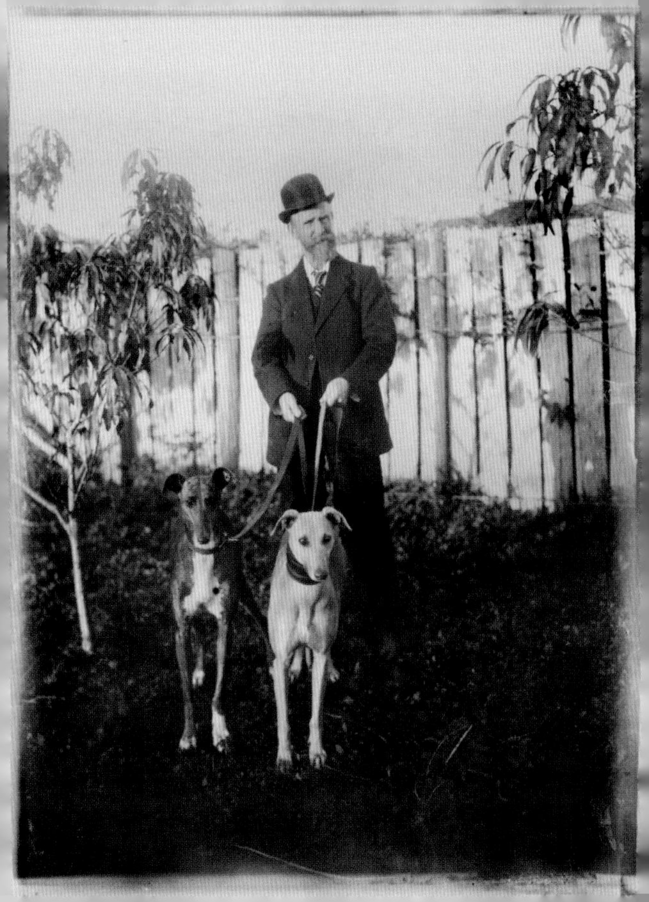

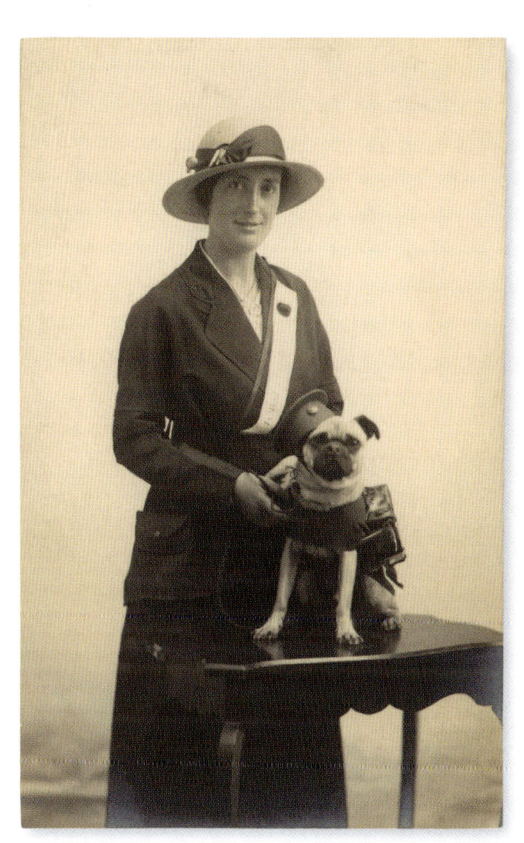

The military dog

Paddy the Irish terrier was the mascot of the 7th (Wellington West Coast) Regiment, based in Whanganui. At the outbreak of the First World War, a company of the regiment was folded into the larger Wellington Infantry Battalion, and when the battalion set sail for Egypt on the *Maunganui* in October 1914, not long after war was declared, Paddy was on board.

He had been smuggled onto the ship by some of the troops, who managed to persuade their officers to make him an official mascot once he was discovered. Paddy landed at Gallipoli with the Australian and New Zealand Army Corps on 25 April 1915. He was often at the front line at Gallipoli, and took part in several charges. The Wellington Battalion suffered terrible losses at Chunuk Bair, but Paddy made it through. When the Second Wellington Battalion was formed shortly afterwards, he went with it to the Western Front, and was on the parade ground at Vauchelles on 30 June 1918 when Prime Minister William Massey inspected troops and this photograph was taken.

Paddy was frequently in the news, and so well loved that after the war the regiment tried to have him brought back home. Alas, as the result of a long-running rabies outbreak, this was not possible, and Paddy was given a new home in Devon, where he died in 1929. His owner sent his collar back to New Zealand, to be looked after by the Wellington Regiment.

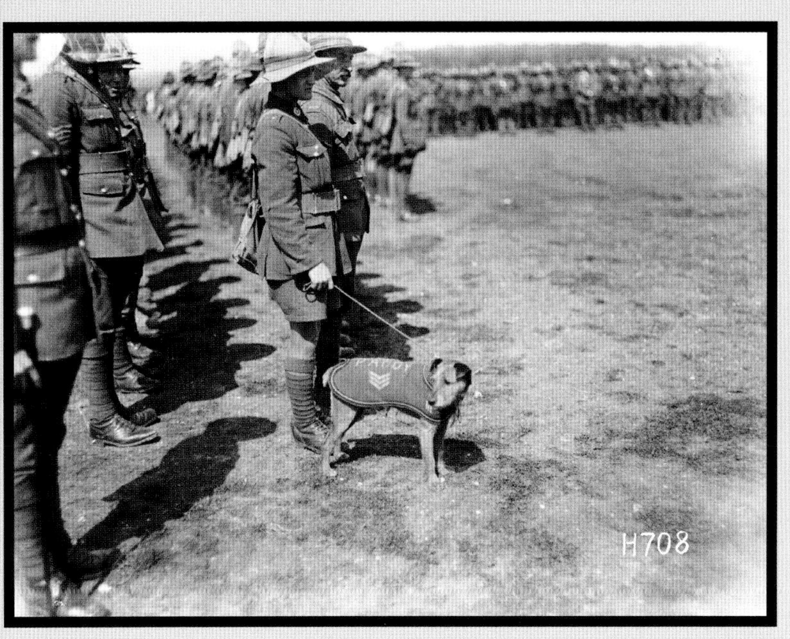
H708

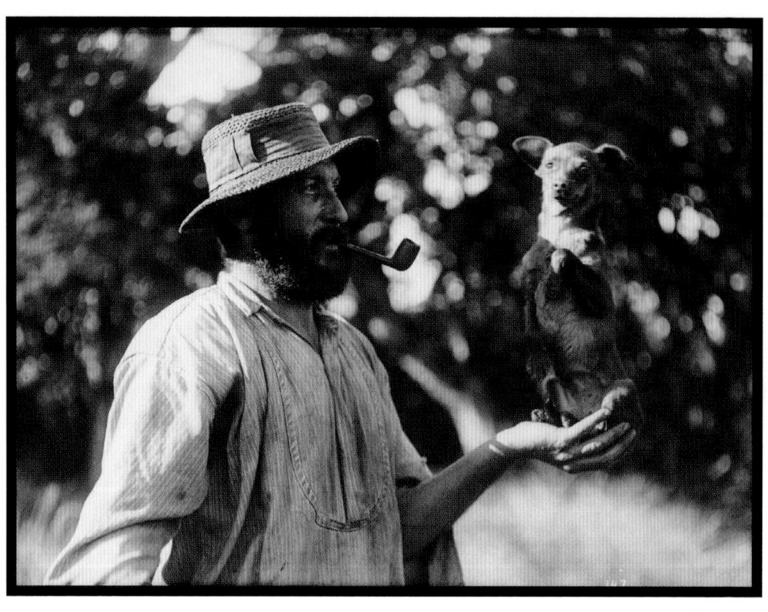

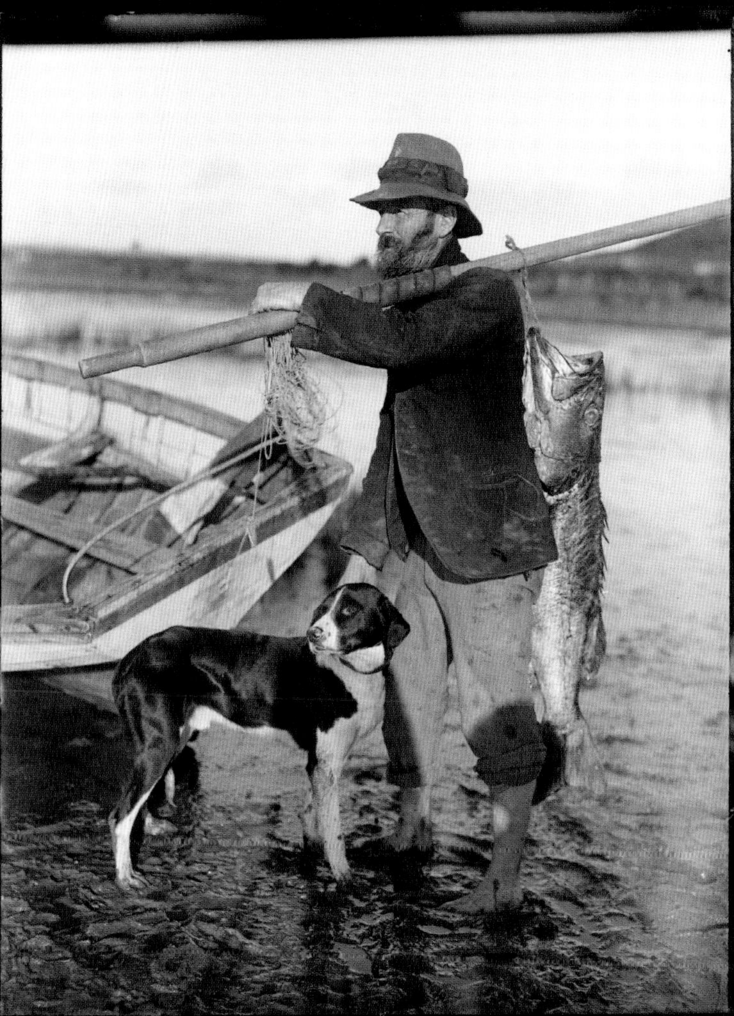

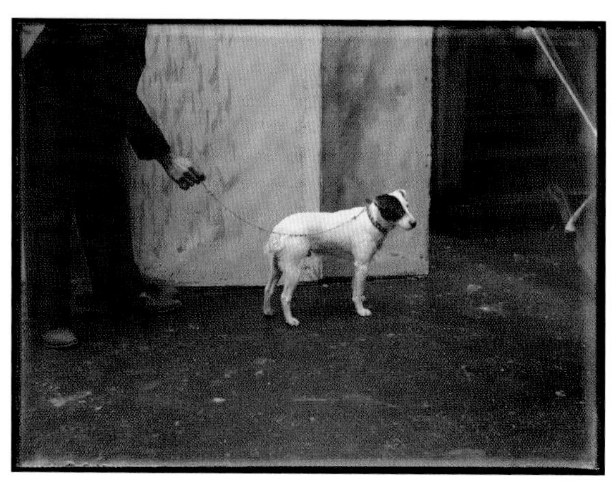

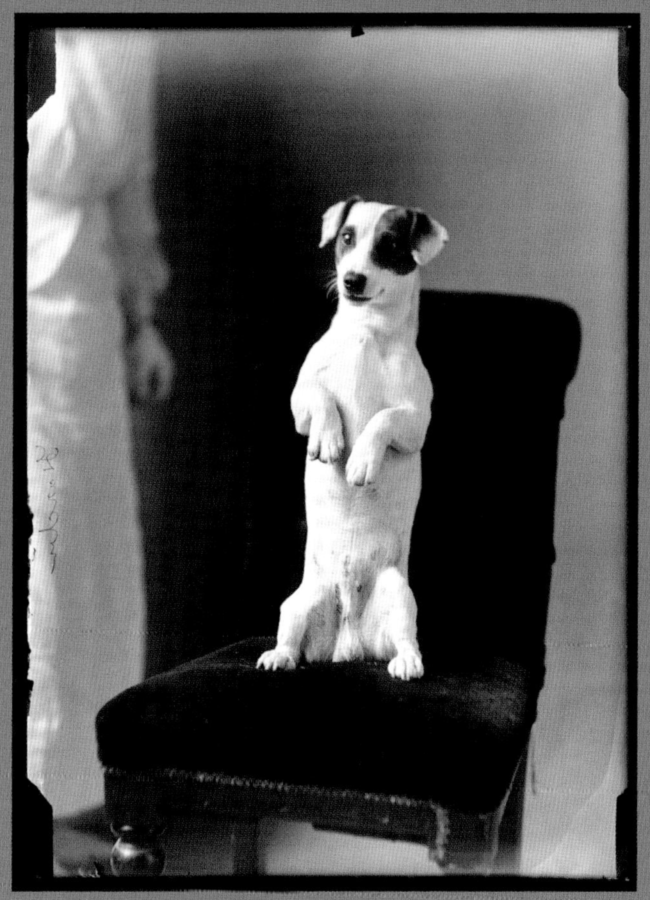

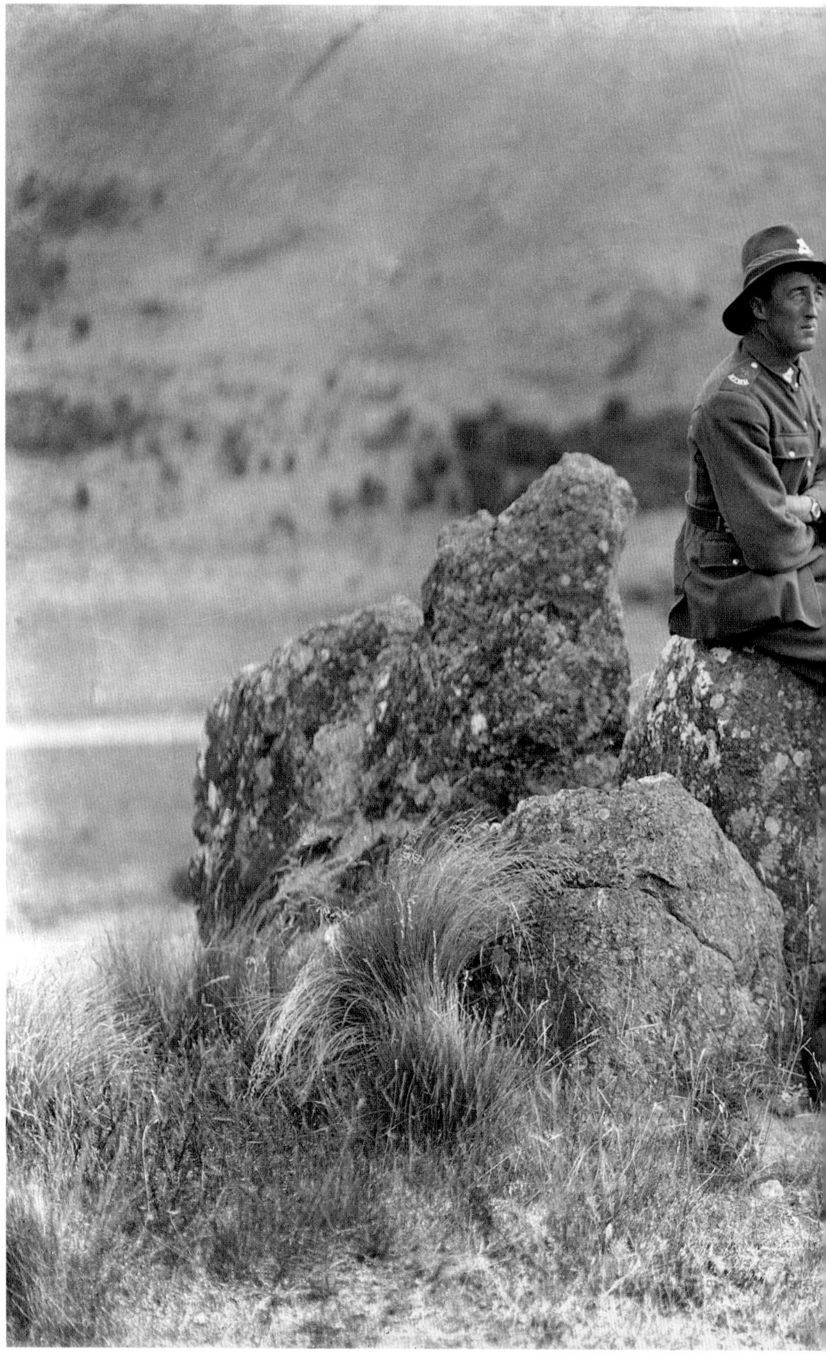

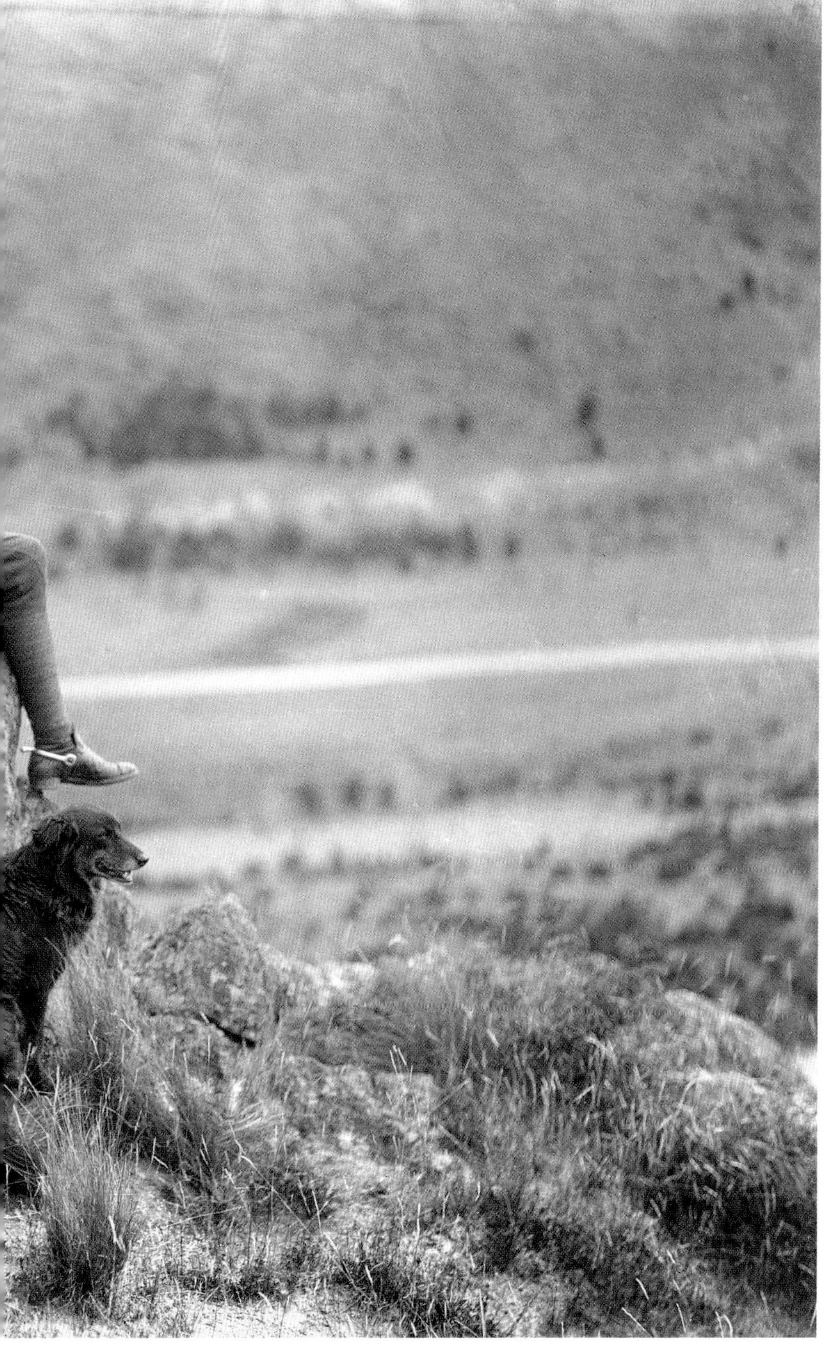

The rugby mascot dog

When the New Zealand Army rugby team toured several English cities in 1917, Floss the fox terrier was its popular mascot. Her owner, the team's driver Percy (Ike) Lowndes, had acquired her from kennels in Towbridge and had taught her many tricks – she could pray, go to bed, play the piano, count to five, sit at a table and give the waiter orders, and take cover in a Zeppelin raid. She toured in a black jersey with a white 'Z' (of 'NZ') and raised hundreds of pounds for disabled service people.

Despite a petition signed by a thousand members of the New Zealand Expeditionary Force, the quarantine authorities would not allow Floss into her adopted nation at the end of the war. Nevertheless, Lowndes smuggled her back with him to Wellington, and after nine months' quarantine on Matiu Somes Island she was a New Zealander.

Floss continued to perform around the North Island for charity. Following her death around 1935, aged an impressive seventeen, she was taxidermied and kept in a glass case in Eastbourne. Floss was later given to the Royal New Zealand Returned and Services' Association, but it is unclear where Floss is today.

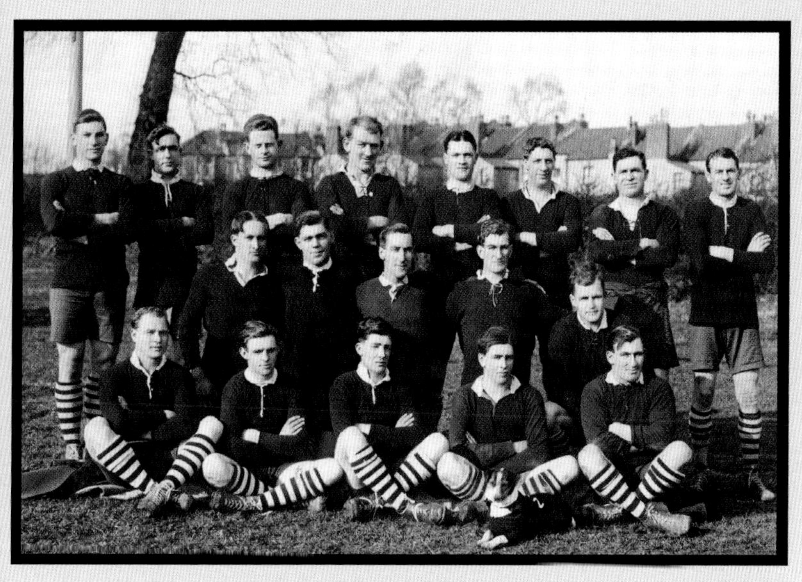

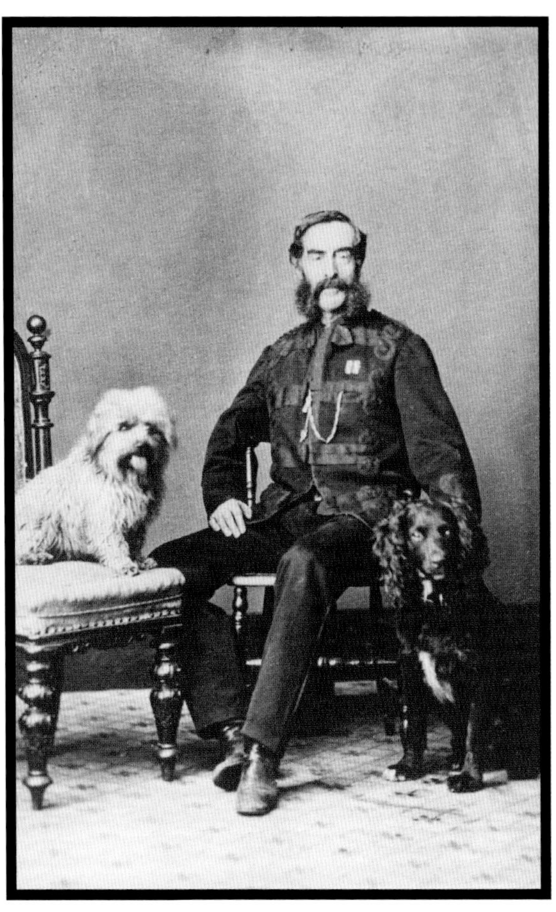

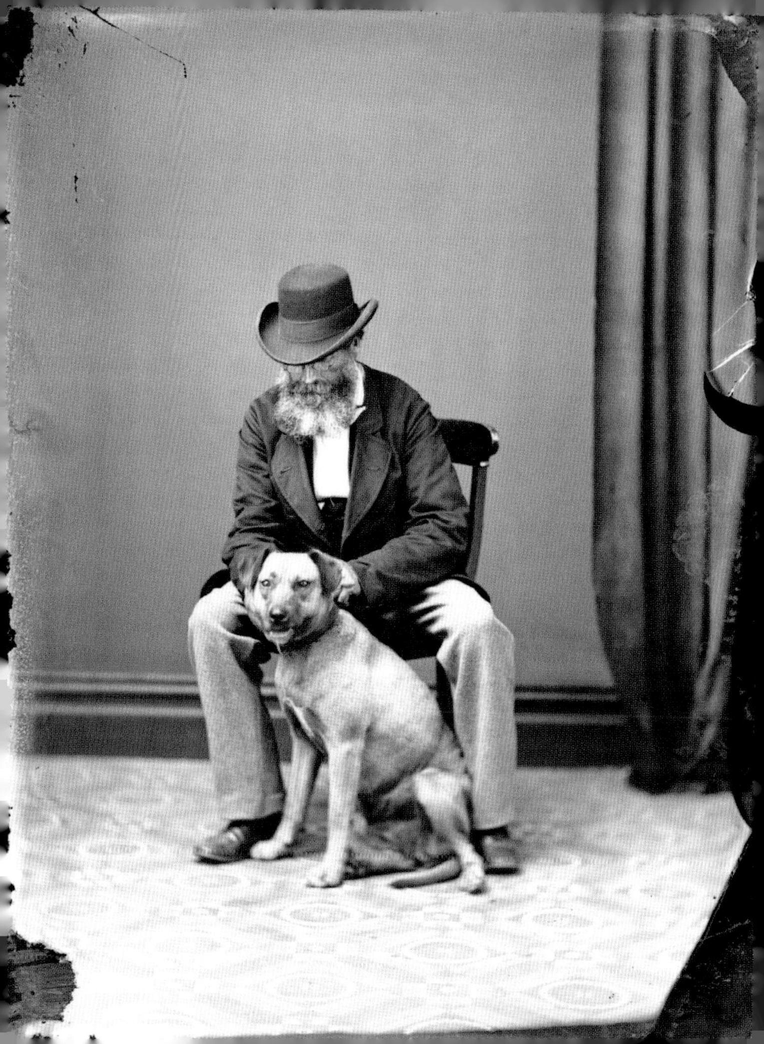

The photographer: The Northwood Brothers

The photographer of this 1910 image of an unidentified woman harvesting grain was Arthur James Northwood. Encouraged by their father, Arthur and his younger brothers Richard and Charles all took courses in photography and accountancy, eventually setting up their own studios across the Northland region, in Auckland and in Gisborne.

Arthur established a studio in Kaitāia in 1910 and Richard and Charles ran the Northwood Brothers Studio in nearby Kohukohu from 1910 to 1919. Charles then opened his own studio in Gisborne in the early 1920s and later established the Bellwood Studios in Queen Street, Auckland. After twenty years managing the Maori Affairs store in Te Kao, Richard joined his older brother at his Kaitāia studio. Arthur died in 1949, but the studio continued to operate as Highlite Studio until 2001.

The Northwoods left a significant documentary legacy of the Far North, especially of the gum industry. The Alexander Turnbull Library holds over 800 original negatives of the brothers' work in a collection called 'Photographs of Northland', the bulk of the images being taken between 1910 and the 1930s by Arthur. Other images from this collection are on pages 65 and 123.

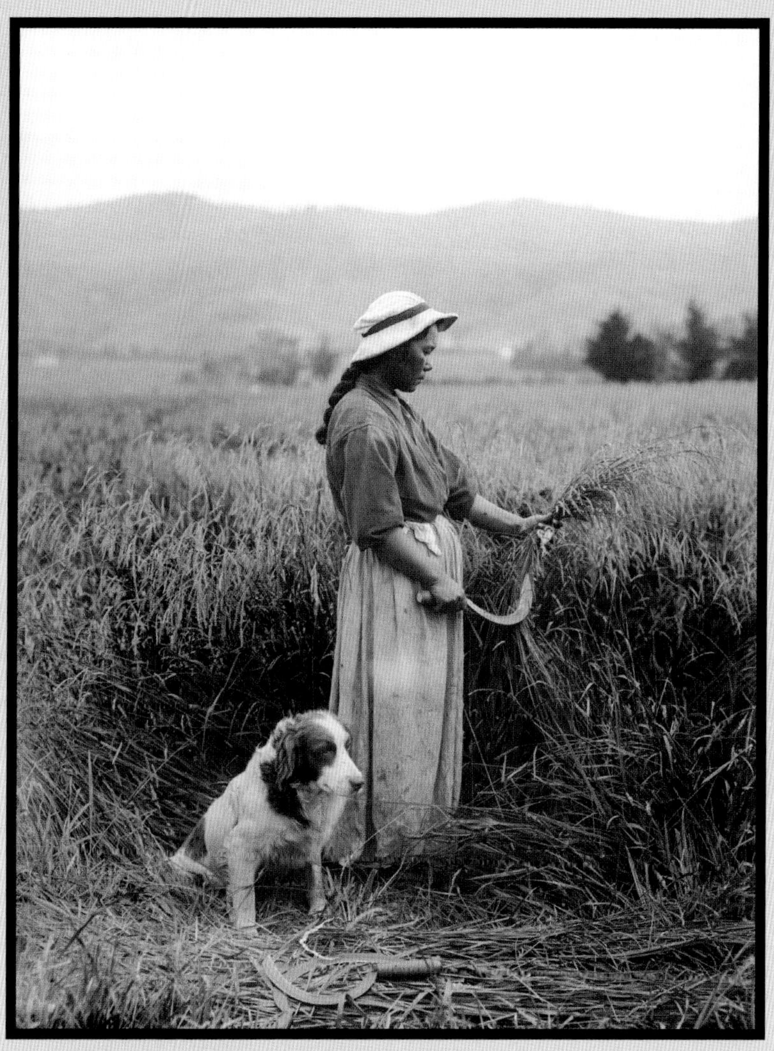

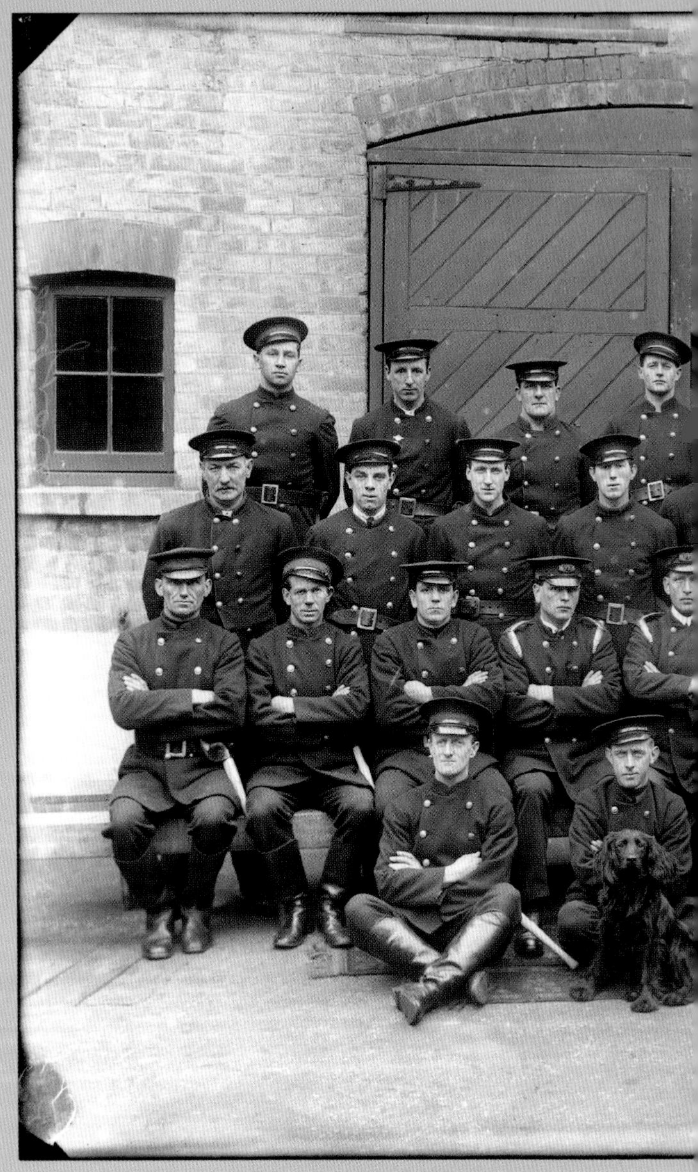

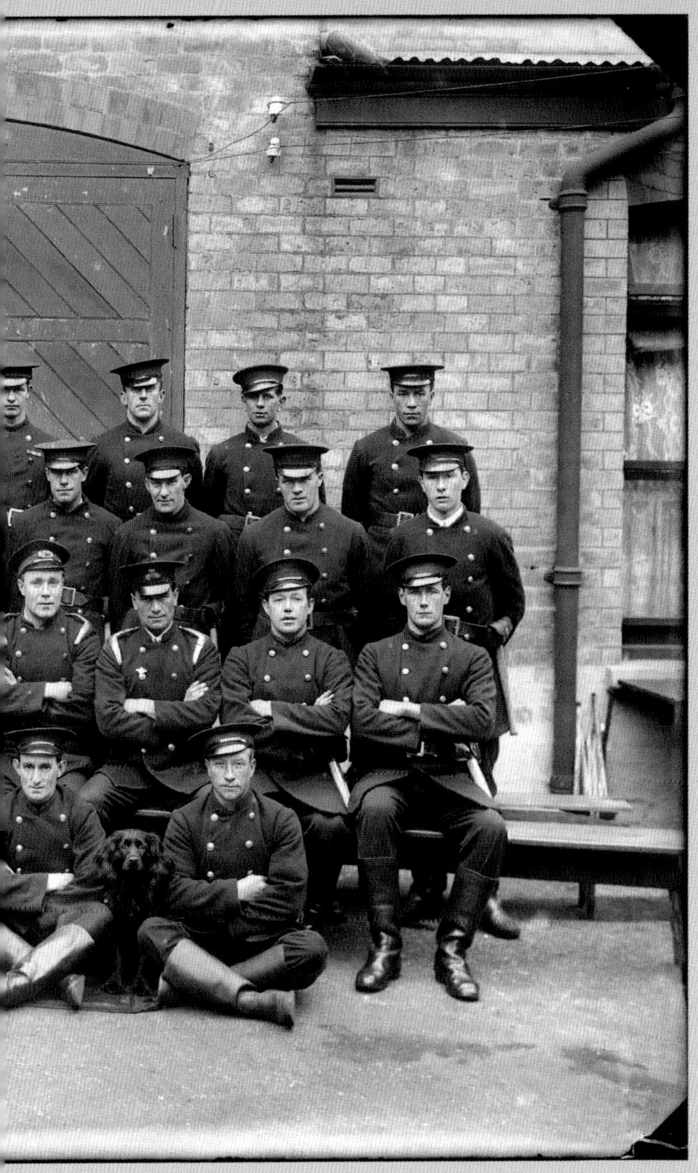

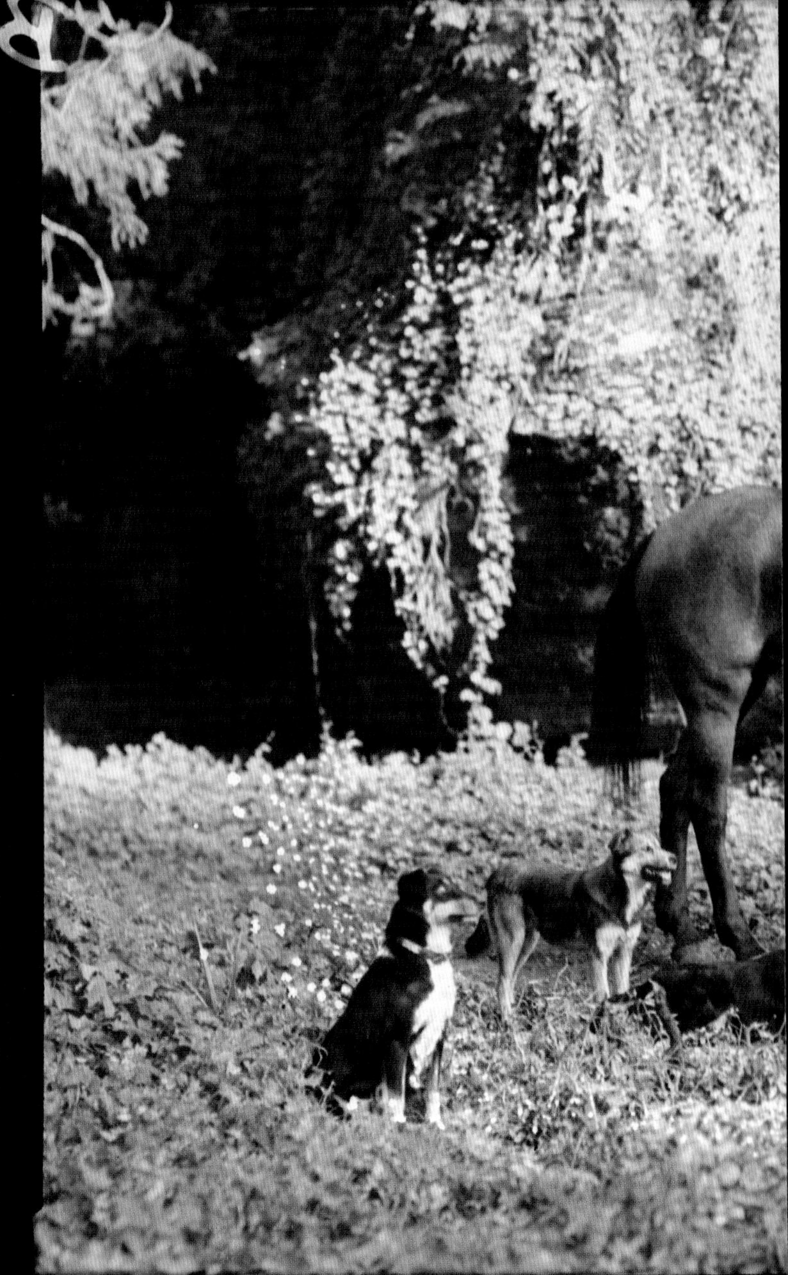

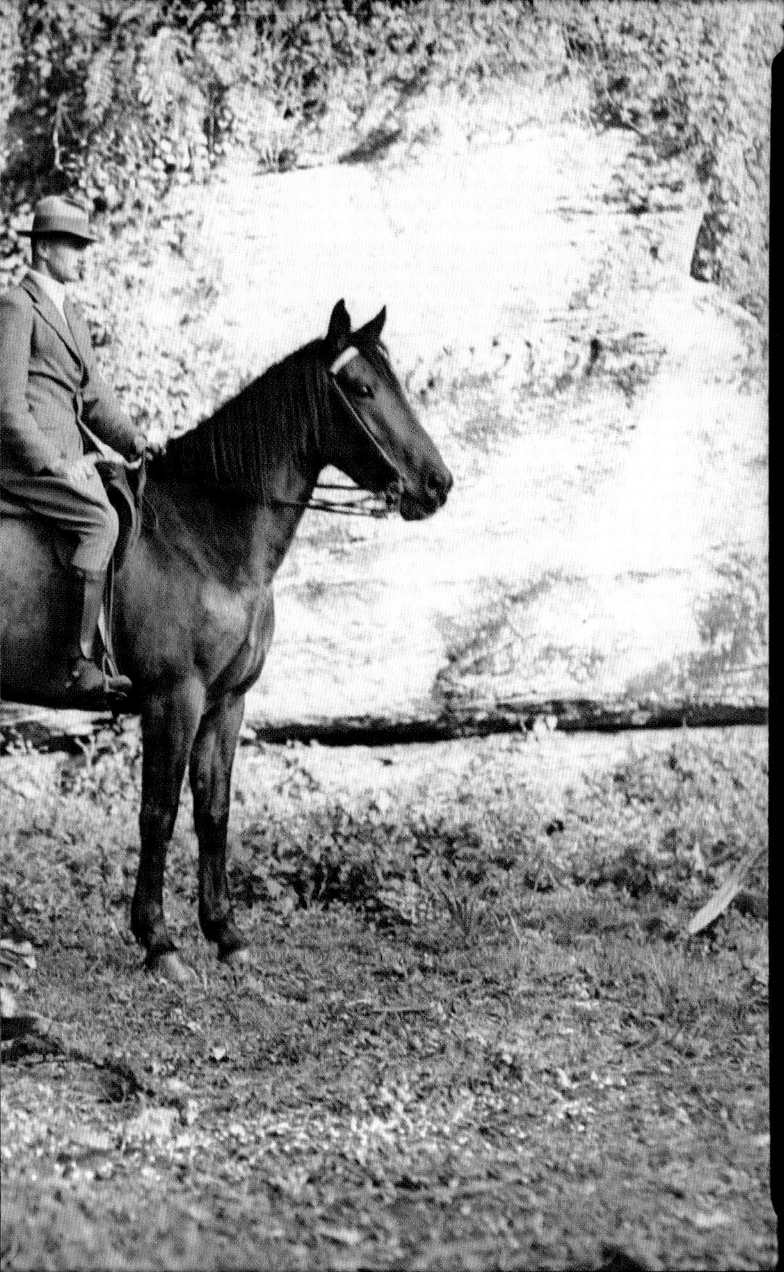

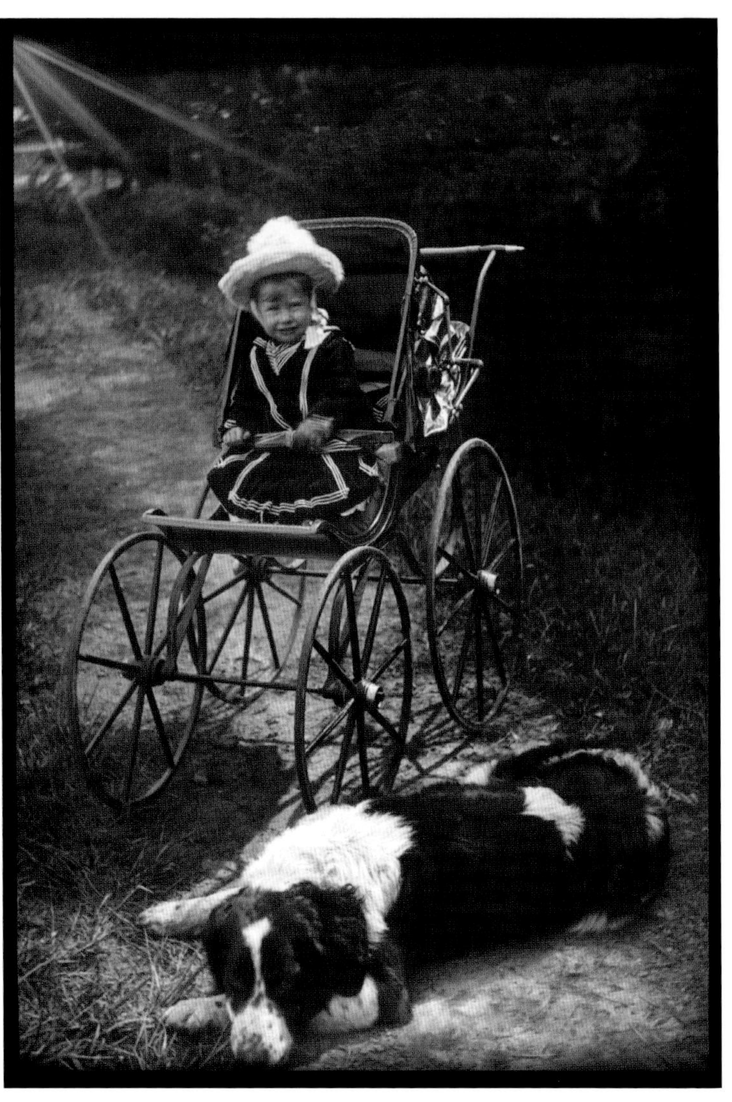

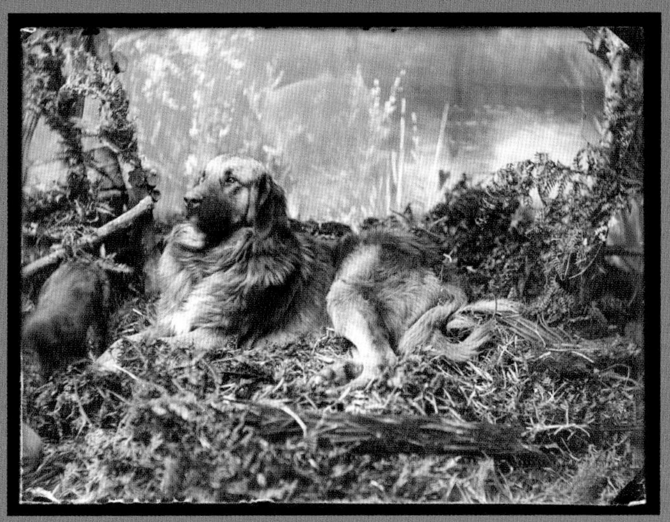

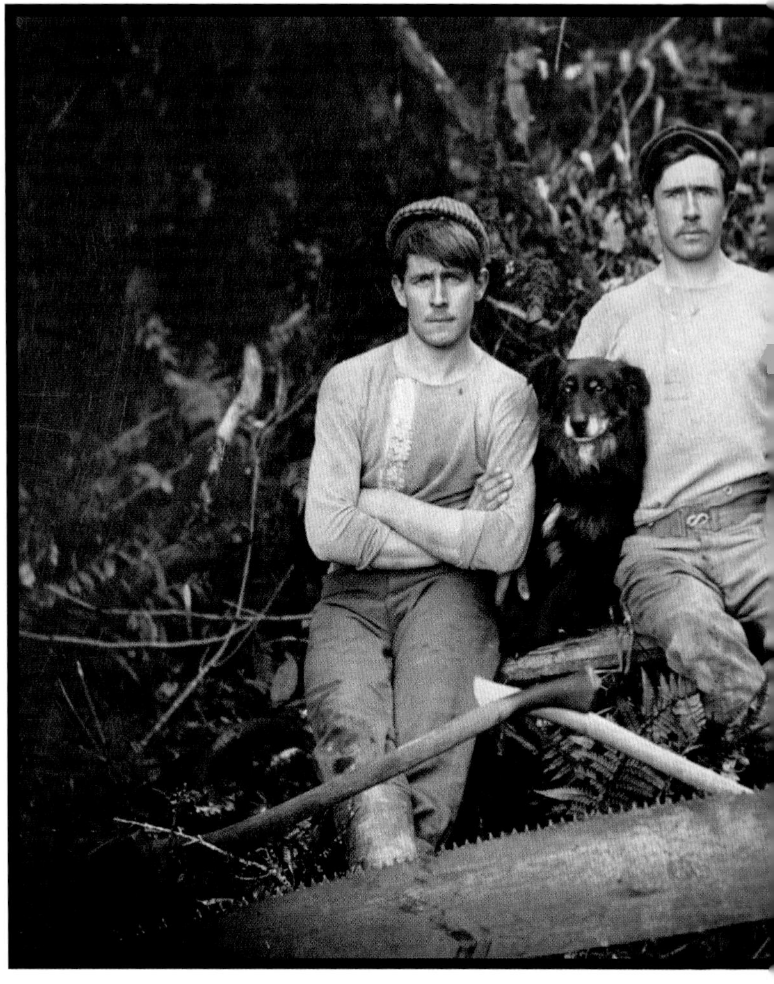

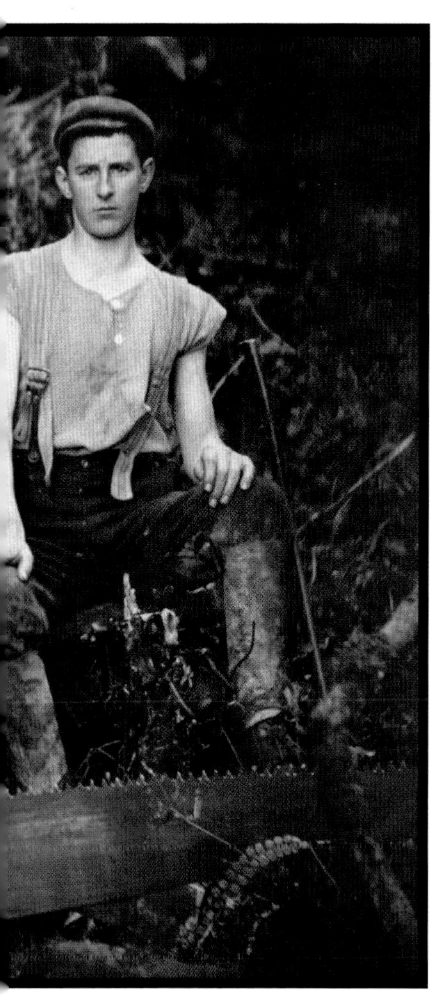

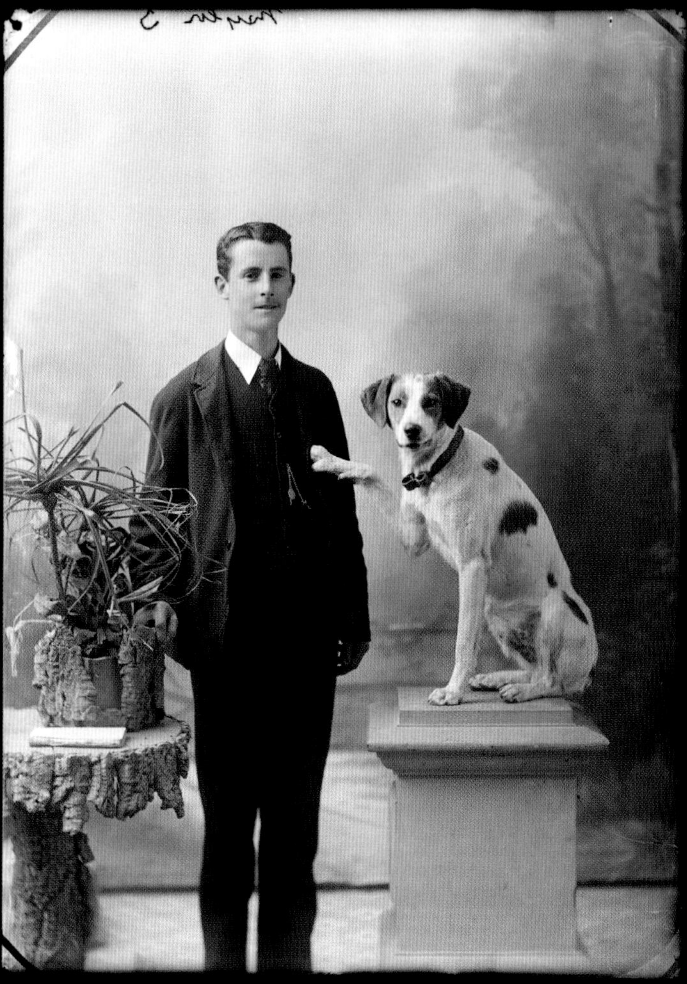

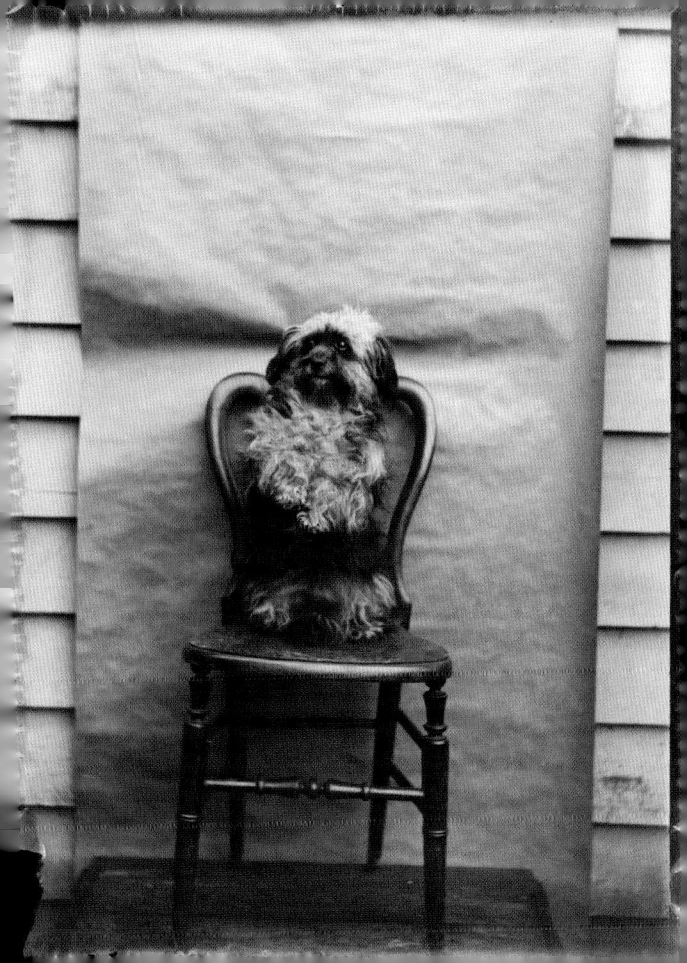

Index of images

Some of the photographs in this book were given proper titles by the photographer or, later, by a museum curator. When institutions inherited glass-plate negatives from photography studios, sometimes all they had was the surname of a subject. Sometimes there was no title at all, and that's where descriptive titles, such as 'Dog reading newspaper', have been used. Some titles have changed over time as more information, such as names, dates, photographers and locations, has been discovered. The varied titles of these 143 photographs reflect this evolution, and where possible we have tried to add more to the story behind the image or the photographer.

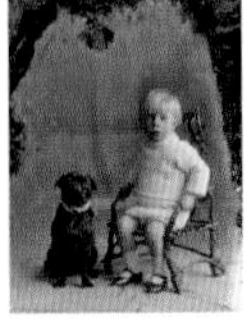

2. Full length portrait of Master Montgomery, sitting on a chair (1913), Schmidt studios.

AUCKLAND LIBRARIES HERITAGE COLLECTIONS, 31-74818

Brothers Herman (1872–1959) and Bernhard Schmidt bought and renamed the Auckland studio of Herman's former employer, Hemus & Hanna, in 1907. The high-profile studio, noted for its portraits of governors and other leading figures, had a large staff, including family members such as Herman's daughter, Muriel. Herman Schmidt won many awards and was made a Fellow of the Royal Photographic Society in 1937. In 1970, around 26,000 half-plate and whole-plate Schmidt Studios negatives were discovered and are now held by the Auckland Libraries Sir George Grey Special Collections.

See also pages 134–135.

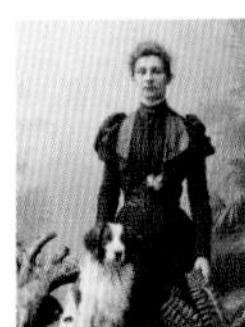

14. Miss Fowler, Tyree studio.

NELSON PROVINCIAL MUSEUM, 41287

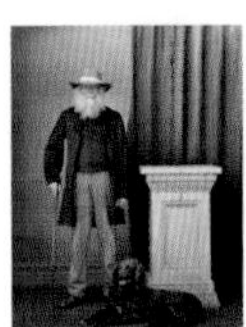

15. Unidentified man with dog (1870s), William J Harding Studio.

ALEXANDER TURNBULL LIBRARY, 1/4-006385-G

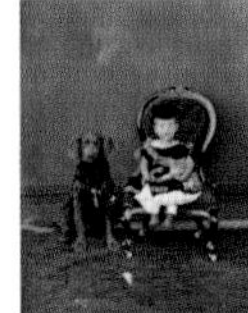

16. Daughter of the Thomlinson family with pet dog (1870–1889), William J Harding Studio.

ALEXANDER TURNBULL LIBRARY, 1/4-030195-G

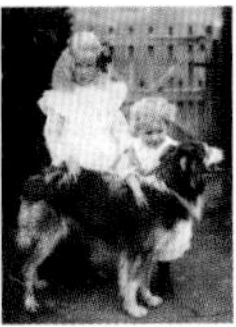

17. Untitled (Portrait of two children with a dog), date unknown, Robert L Lockerbie.

COLLECTION OF THE SOUTHLAND MUSEUM AND ART GALLERY NIHO O TE TANIWHA. GIFT OF JOAN WELLS, 2005. 2006.39.66

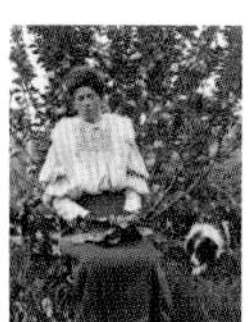

18. Woman and dog (1900–1932), William J Young.
MANAWATŪ HERITAGE, 2015G_YOUNG105_010225

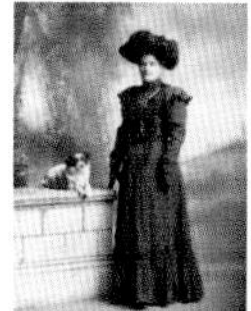

25. Mrs Coley and a dog (*c.*1905), James McAllister.
ALEXANDER TURNBULL LIBRARY, 1/2-034383-G

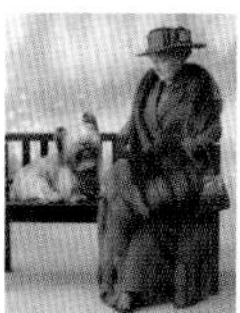

19. Mrs J Harris with dog (*c.*1915), H H Clifford.
CANTERBURY MUSEUM, 1980.175.26587

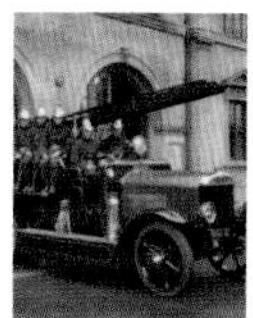

26–27. Firemen and fire engine, Whanganui (1926), Tesla Studios.
ALEXANDER TURNBULL LIBRARY, 1/1-017502-F

The Tesla Studios, named for the inventor Nikola Tesla, were opened in Whanganui by Mark Lampe in 1908 and ran until his retirement in 1955. The studio's thousands of glass-plate and film negatives are held by both the Alexander Turnbull Library and the Whanganui Regional Museum.

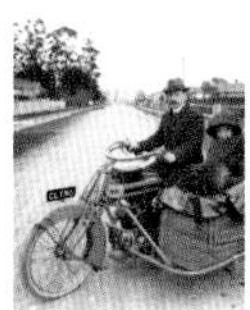

20–21. Clyno motorcycle (*c.*1920), *The Press.*
ALEXANDER TURNBULL LIBRARY, 1/1-008536-G

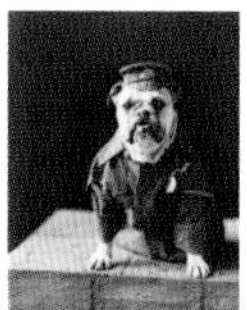

22. Mayo dog, Tyree studio.
NELSON PROVINCIAL MUSEUM, 90051

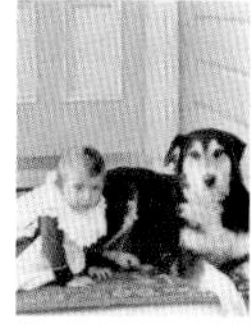

28. Lucy Shailer and dog [Jumbo] (*c.*1889), George W Shailer.
MANAWATŪ HERITAGE, 2015P_P1627_012500
See also pages 42–43.

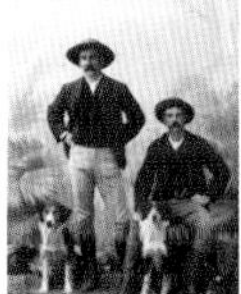

23. Mr Oldham, Tyree studio.
NELSON PROVINCIAL MUSEUM, 41115

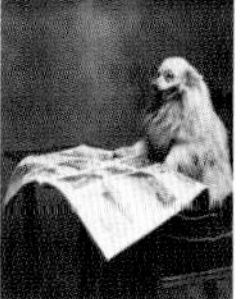

29. Dog reading newspaper, F N Jones.
NELSON PROVINCIAL MUSEUM, 313849

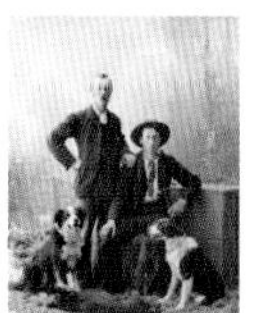

24. Whiting, Tyree studio.
NELSON PROVINCIAL MUSEUM, 47920

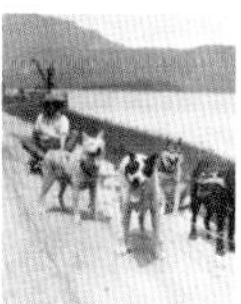

31. Training the dogs on Quail Island in Lyttelton Harbour (1911), James R Dennistoun.
CANTERBURY MUSEUM, 1969.61.22
See story, page 30.

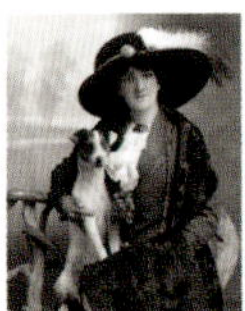

32. Mrs Hanby (1900s), Tyree studio.

Nelson Provincial Museum, 82860

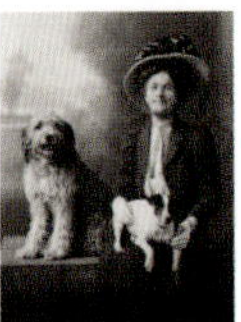

33. Mrs Churton (1900s), Tyree studio.

Nelson Provincial Museum, 77662

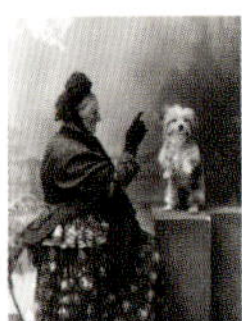

34. Mrs Harris and dog, Tyree studio.

Nelson Provincial Museum, 45017

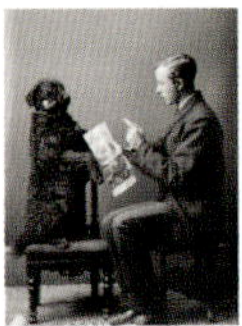

35, front cover. Mr Canavan (1882), unknown photographer.

Nelson Provincial Museum, W E Brown Collection, 16583

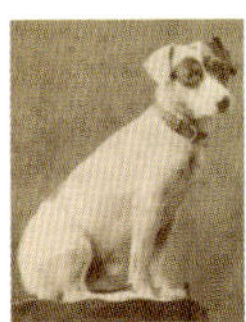

36. Small dog, *c.*1870, Dunedin, Burton Brothers studio.

Te Papa, O.034227

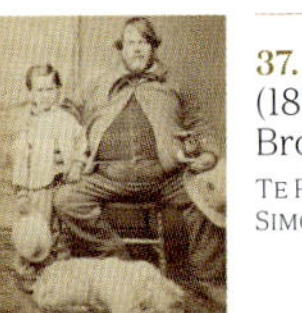

37. Man, boy and dog (1870–74), Nicholas Brothers.

Te Papa, O.043334. Gift of Simon Knight, 2015

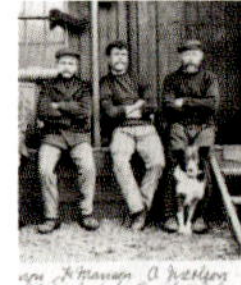

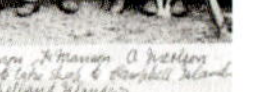

39. Shetland Island farmers, Campbell Island (*c.*1904), Karl Gerstenkorm.

Alexander Turnbull Library, 1/2-114162-F

See story, page 38.

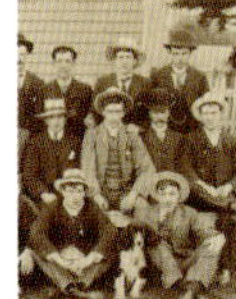

40–41. Dunedin rugby club prior to travelling to an out of town game, unknown photographer.

Toitū Otago Settlers Museum, E445

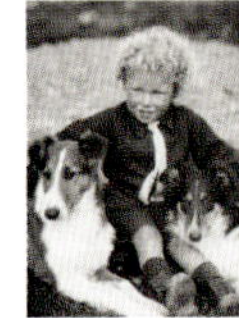

42–43. Sid Shailer and Dogs (c.1912–1914), George W Shailer.

Manawatū Heritage, 2013G_P1618_006818

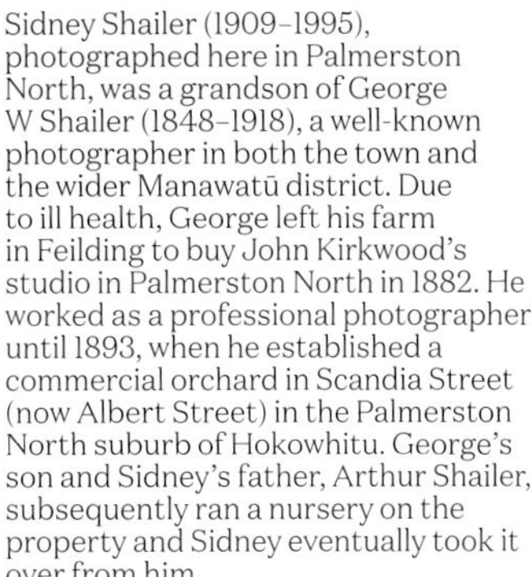

Sidney Shailer (1909–1995), photographed here in Palmerston North, was a grandson of George W Shailer (1848–1918), a well-known photographer in both the town and the wider Manawatū district. Due to ill health, George left his farm in Feilding to buy John Kirkwood's studio in Palmerston North in 1882. He worked as a professional photographer until 1893, when he established a commercial orchard in Scandia Street (now Albert Street) in the Palmerston North suburb of Hokowhitu. George's son and Sidney's father, Arthur Shailer, subsequently ran a nursery on the property and Sidney eventually took it over from him.

See also page 28.

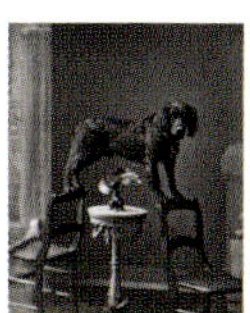

44. Stanton dog, Theodor Bloch.
NELSON PROVINCIAL MUSEUM, 4344

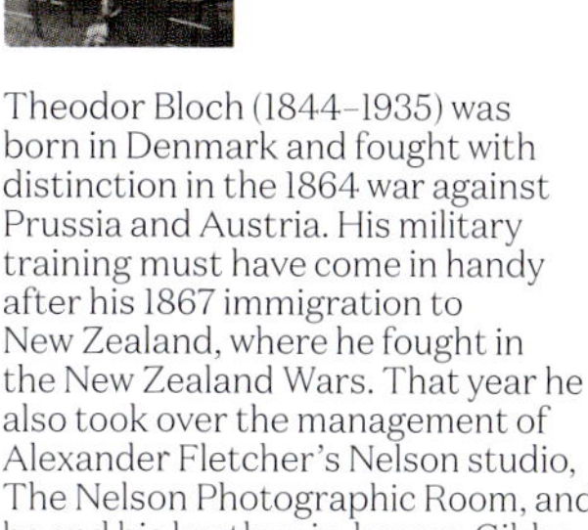

Theodor Bloch (1844–1935) was born in Denmark and fought with distinction in the 1864 war against Prussia and Austria. His military training must have come in handy after his 1867 immigration to New Zealand, where he fought in the New Zealand Wars. That year he also took over the management of Alexander Fletcher's Nelson studio, The Nelson Photographic Room, and he and his brother-in-law ran Gibbs & Bloch in Trafalgar Street, Nelson, throughout the 1870s. The Nelson Museum has 2500 of his negatives and several hundred of his original prints. See also pages 45 and 67.

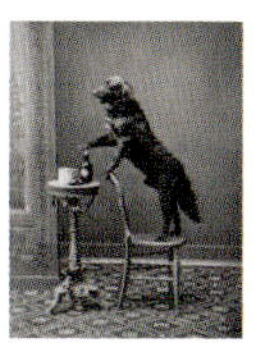

45. Stanton dog, Theodor Bloch.
NELSON PROVINCIAL MUSEUM, 4650

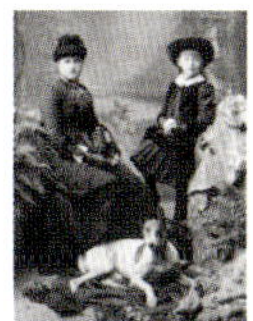

46. McConchie, Tyree studio.
NELSON PROVINCIAL MUSEUM, 29156

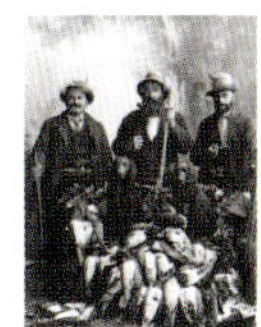

47. Fairey and Plum shooting party (*c.*1900), Tyree studio.
NELSON PROVINCIAL MUSEUM, 176893

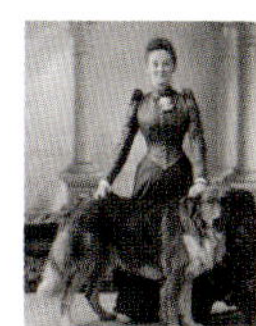

48. Miss Collins and dog, Tyree studio.
NELSON PROVINCIAL MUSEUM, 44745

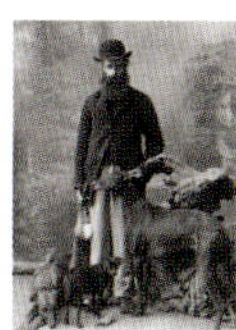

49. Mr Grey and dogs, Tyree studio.
NELSON PROVINCIAL MUSEUM, 21424

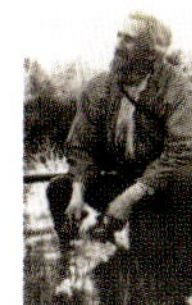

51. Douglas with his inseparable Betsey Jane (1894), Arthur P Harper.
ALEXANDER TURNBULL LIBRARY, 75-241-001C-17

See story, page 50.

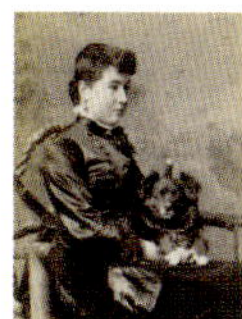

52. Agnes Grey Bannerman (later Mrs John Reid Wilson) and dog (1880s), unknown photographer.
TOITŪ OTAGO SETTLERS MUSEUM, A523

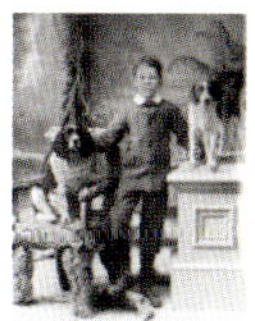

53. Shallcross, Tyree studio.
NELSON PROVINCIAL MUSEUM, 20201

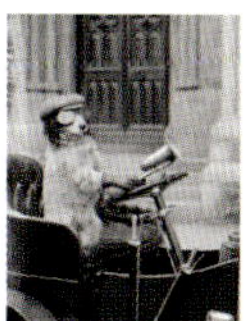

54. Dog at the wheel of a car (1920s), unknown photographer.
ALEXANDER TURNBULL LIBRARY, 1/2-073999-G

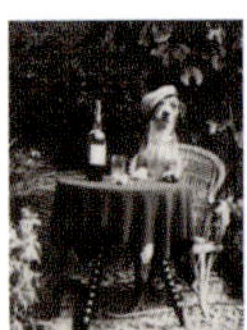

55. Dog with a hat on, sitting on a chair at a small table, unknown photographer.
NELSON PROVINCIAL MUSEUM, 318674

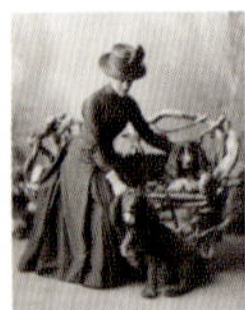

56. Kennedy, Tyree studio.
NELSON PROVINCIAL MUSEUM, 46329

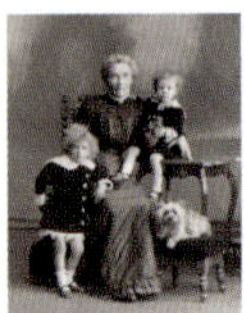

57. Sinclair family with small dog (*c.*1920), Berry & Co.
TE PAPA, B.047287

Berry & Co. was established in 1899 and operated on Cuba Street in Welllington until *c.*1930. It is perhaps best known for the more than one hundred portraits it took of soldiers before they set off for the battlefields of the First World War, and for specialising in taking images using the natural lighting of its studio. The Berry & Co. name survives on the façade of 147 Cuba Street.

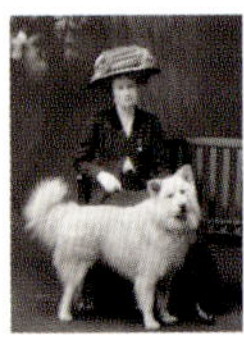

59. Miss Beatrice Curlett and Erebus (*c.*1909), H H Clifford.
CANTERBURY MUSEUM, 1980.175.21122

See story, page 58.

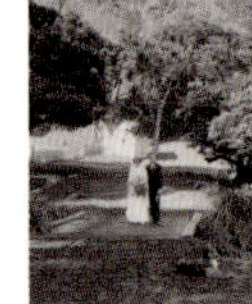

60–61. A bridal couple and dog, unknown photographer.
AUCKLAND LIBRARIES HERITAGE COLLECTIONS, 255A-7412

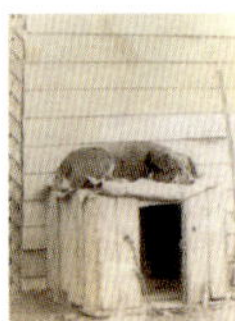

62. Dog sleeping on top of dog house (1896).
CULTURE WAITAKI, 2014/45.02.046

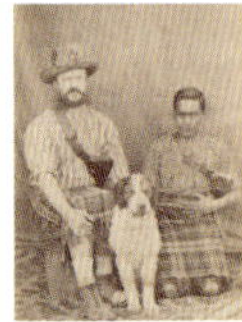

63. Two men with a dog (1860–1880), unknown photographer.
TE PAPA, O.041473

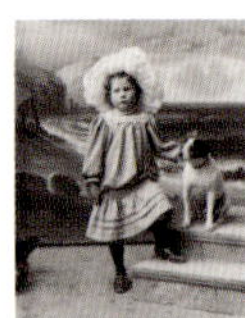

64. McDowell, Tyree studio.
NELSON PROVINCIAL MUSEUM, 71004

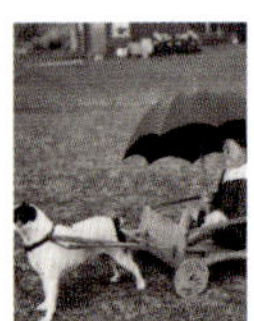

65. Boy in dog-drawn cart (*c.*1910), Arthur J Northwood.
ALEXANDER TURNBULL LIBRARY, 1/1-006229-G

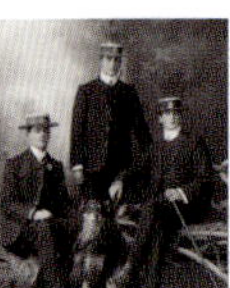

66. Livick, Tyree studio.
NELSON PROVINCIAL MUSEUM, 68118

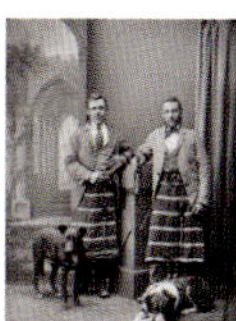

67. Marius, Theodor Bloch.
NELSON PROVINCIAL MUSEUM, 5240

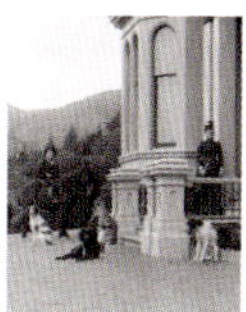

68–69. Watt's House – later Adams house, Melrose, Adams group, Tyree studio.
NELSON PROVINCIAL MUSEUM, 178632

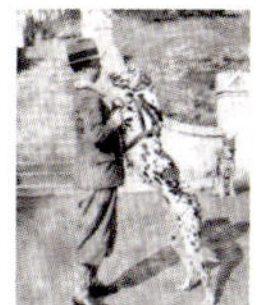

70. Tuckfield man, A R Kingsford.
NELSON PROVINCIAL MUSEUM, 162290

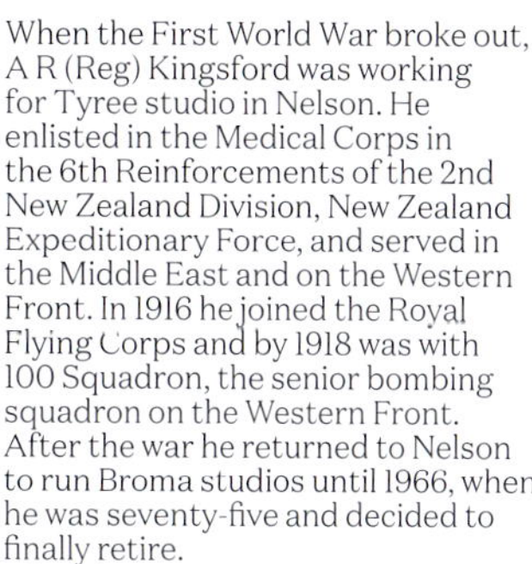

When the First World War broke out, A R (Reg) Kingsford was working for Tyree studio in Nelson. He enlisted in the Medical Corps in the 6th Reinforcements of the 2nd New Zealand Division, New Zealand Expeditionary Force, and served in the Middle East and on the Western Front. In 1916 he joined the Royal Flying Corps and by 1918 was with 100 Squadron, the senior bombing squadron on the Western Front. After the war he returned to Nelson to run Broma studios until 1966, when he was seventy-five and decided to finally retire.

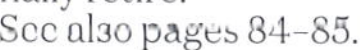

See also pages 84–85.

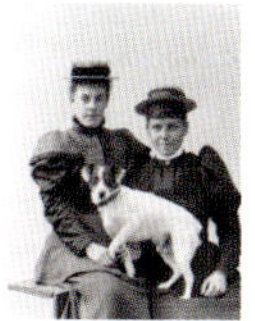

71. Buchanan, Tyree studio.
NELSON PROVINCIAL MUSEUM, 46138

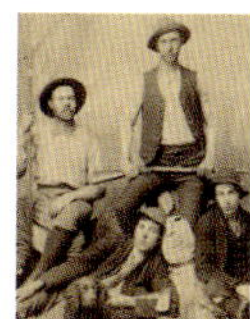

72–73. Tramping group, 1889, unknown photographer.
TOITŪ OTAGO SETTLERS MUSEUM, D373

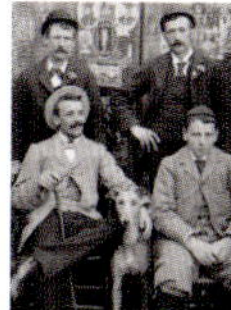

74. Men, boy, and a dog (*c.*1910), Arthur James Woodhouse.
ALEXANDER TURNBULL LIBRARY, 1/2-096442-G

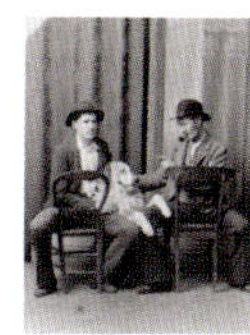

75. Mr Gren and Mr Collie, seated with a dog (1888), William J Harding Studio.
ALEXANDER TURNBULL LIBRARY, 1/4-004739-G

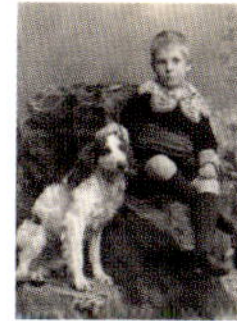

77. Anthony Wilding with the family dog Carlo (1889), unknown photographer.
CANTERBURY MUSEUM, 1989.147.370

See story, page 76.

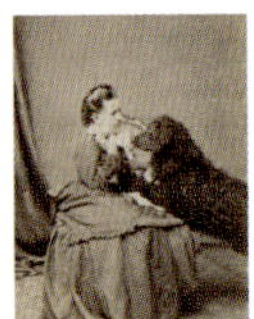

78. Daisy Milford and Terror (1870s), unknown photographer.
CANTERBURY MUSEUM, ALBUM 39

Terror belonged to the Hargreaves family of Lyttelton. Through the 1870s Annie Hargreaves kept a series of diaries that recorded visits to Tīmaru and throughout New Zealand. The family dog Terror, who may have been a curly-coated retriever, makes a regular appearance in its pages. On at least one trip to Tīmaru in 1874, Annie took him to Thomas Price's photography studio, where his portrait was taken with Annie and her friends. In this photograph, Terror is jumping up to investigate something held by Annie's friend Daisy Milford.

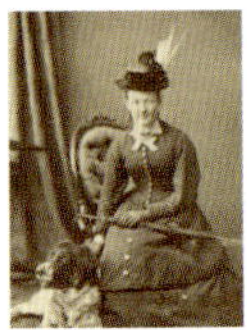

79. Mrs Sealy and Sailor-boy (1870s), unknown photographer.
CANTERBURY MUSEUM, ALBUM 39

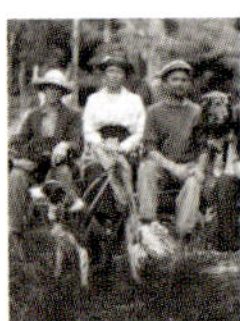

80–81. Group with dogs (1900–1915), unknown photographer.
AUCKLAND WAR MEMORIAL MUSEUM TĀMAKI PAENGA HIRA, PH-2019-13-8-19

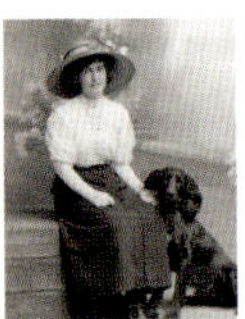

82. Miss Harden, Tyree studio.
NELSON PROVINCIAL MUSEUM, 84364

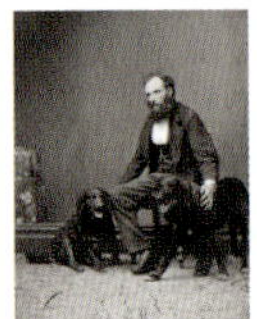

83. Unidentified man, seated, accompanied by two dogs (1870–1890), William J Harding Studio.
ALEXANDER TURNBULL LIBRARY, 1/4-006471-G

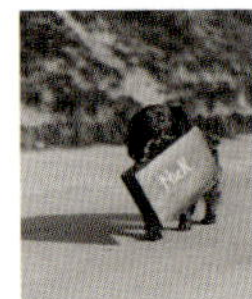

84–85. Spaniel, A R Kingsford.
NELSON PROVINCIAL MUSEUM, 161755

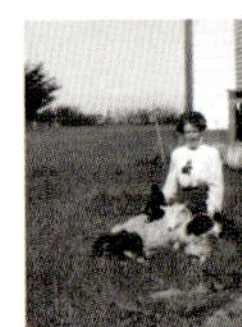

86–87. Woman with dogs and pet sheep (1900–1910), William J Young.
MANAWATŪ HERITAGE, 2015G_YOUNG162_010274

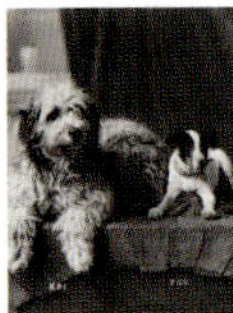

88. Churton, Tyree studio.
NELSON PROVINCIAL MUSEUM, 77663

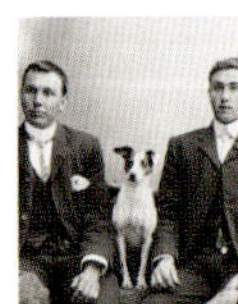

89. Wootten, Tyree studio.
NELSON PROVINCIAL MUSEUM, 65687

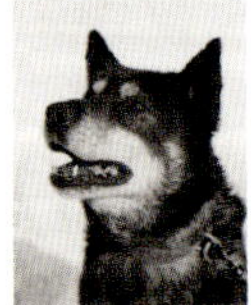

91. Osman, Scott's Best Sledge Dog (*c.*1910), Herbert Ponting.
CANTERBURY MUSEUM, 1975,289

See story, page 90.

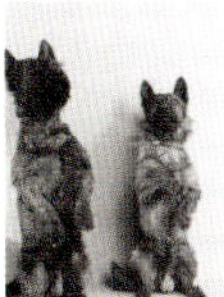

92. Palmer, dogs, Ellis Dudgeon.
NELSON PROVINCIAL MUSEUM, 212125

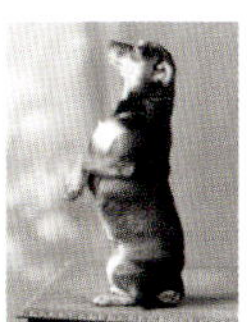

93. Jellyman, dog, Tyree studio.
NELSON PROVINCIAL MUSEUM, 97621

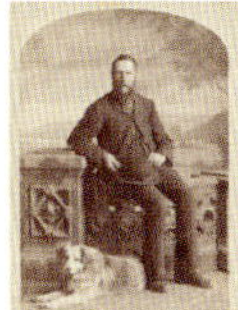

94. Seated man and dog (1880s), Foy Brothers.
TE PAPA, O.025032

The Foy brothers, Joseph (1847–1923) and James (d.1890), ran their eponymous photographers' business in Thames between 1872 and 1909. They specialised in studio portraits for local settler residents; their seventy photographic portraits of local or visiting Māori were taken during Land Court sittings in Thames. The Foys' portraits are a significant record of nineteenth-century New Zealand and of some of the leading individuals of the time.

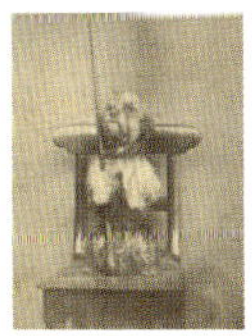

95. Portrait of a dog (1866), A Rayner.
HAWKE'S BAY MUSEUMS TRUST RUAWHARO TĀ-Ū-RANGI, 16681

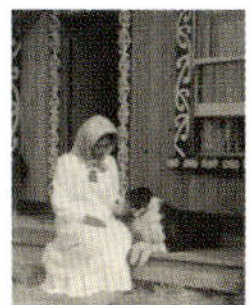

96–97. Mākereti [Thom (Papakura)] at Tukiterangi, Whakarewarewa (1907), Harold Hislop.
ALEXANDER TURNBULL LIBRARY, PA1-O-229-26-4

Mākereti (Te Arawa and Tūhourangi / Ngati Wahiao; 1873–1930) is pictured here in 1907 outside her first whare, Tukiterangi, at Whakarewarewa. By this time she had become well known as 'Maggie Papakura' or 'Guide Maggie', renowned for guiding and running concert parties at the world-famous thermal area. In 1910 she left for Australia and then England, where she married and studied anthropology at Oxford University. Makereti had dogs throughout her life, so this one is likely to have belonged to her. A diary entry from 1907 reads, 'I remember leaving home to attend Hukarere College in Napier. I don't know whether I was sad to leave my parents, or my dear little dog.'

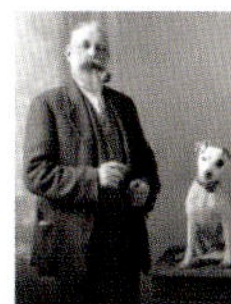

98. Mr Drummond, Tyree studio.
NELSON PROVINCIAL MUSEUM, 93253

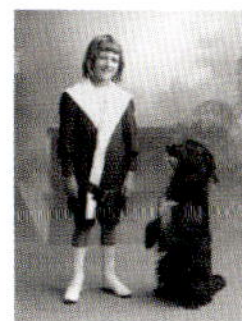

99. Askenbeck boy and dog, Tyree studio.
NELSON PROVINCIAL MUSEUM, 80550

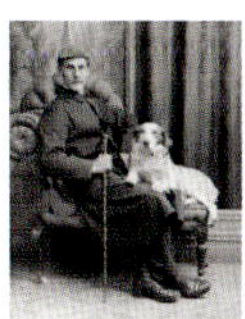

100. Unidentified man, seated, with his dog (1870–1890), William J Harding Studio.
ALEXANDER TURNBULL LIBRARY, 1/4-006490-G

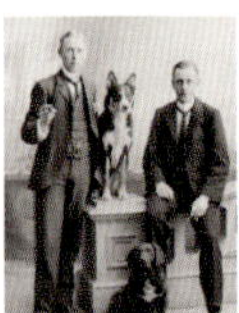

101. Bannehr, Tyree studio.
NELSON PROVINCIAL MUSEUM, 64033

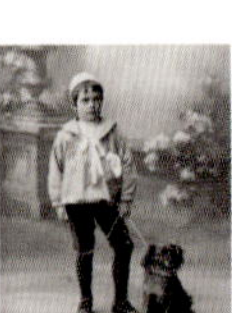

103. Jones, Tyree studio.
NELSON PROVINCIAL MUSEUM, 68113
See story, page 102.

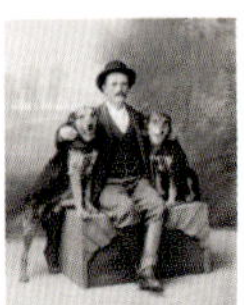

104. Fred Tyree, Tyree studio.
NELSON PROVINCIAL MUSEUM, 70683

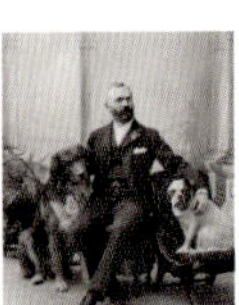

105. Mr Kirkpatrick, Tyree studio.
NELSON PROVINCIAL MUSEUM, 42746

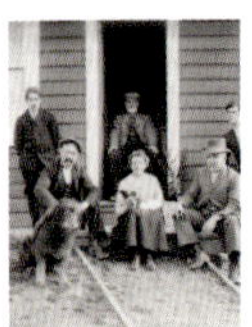

106–107. Untitled (Group portrait), date unknown, Robert L Lockerbie.
COLLECTION OF THE SOUTHLAND MUSEUM AND ART GALLERY NIHO O TE TANIWHA. GIFT OF JOAN WELLS, 2005. 2006.39.308

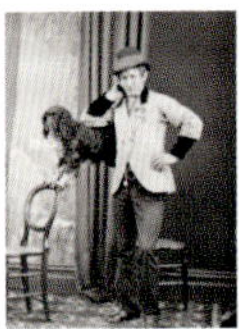

109. Mr Frank and his acrobatic dog (1870–1889), William J Harding Studio.
ALEXANDER TURNBULL LIBRARY, 1/4-030219-G
See story, page 108.

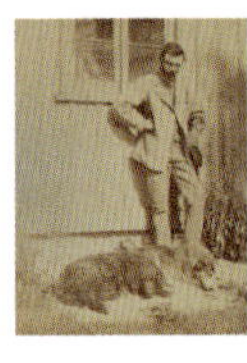

110. Samuel Delabere Barker and the dogs Sambo (left) and Jack (right) (1871), Alfred C Barker.
CANTERBURY MUSEUM, 1958.81.105

One of Canterbury's most interesting early settlers, medical doctor Alfred Charles Barker (1819–1873) turned to photography around 1858, built a dark room, and then devoted the rest of his life to photography. His images of family, events, Christchurch and Canterbury, while often technically flawed, are admired for their sensitivity and form, and are, of course, an extremely valuable historical record. Barker's son Samuel (1848–1901), librarian to the Supreme Court and a talented botanist, was also a photographer, and his images taken in the Chatham Islands in 1873 are regarded as very significant.

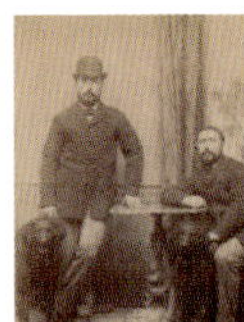

111. From an album owned by the Reid family (1870s), unknown photographer.
TOITŪ OTAGO SETTLERS MUSEUM, ALBUM 139

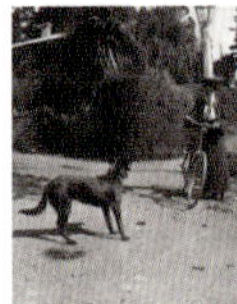

112. Unnamed, unknown photographer.
NELSON PROVINCIAL MUSEUM, 318772

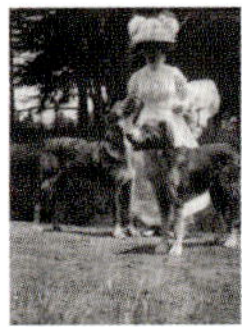

113. Unnamed, unknown photographer.
NELSON PROVINCIAL MUSEUM, 318472

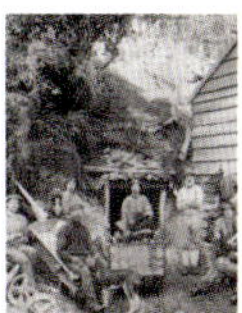

115. Pakawau coal miners, Tyree studio.
NELSON PROVINCIAL MUSEUM, 182109
See story, page 114.

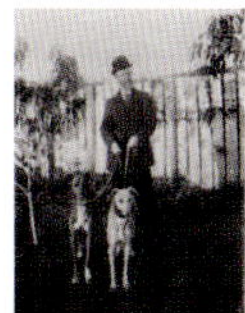

118. Man and two greyhounds, E Bradbury & Co Studio.
WAIKATO MUSEUM TE WHARE TAONGA O WAIKATO, 1961/4/223

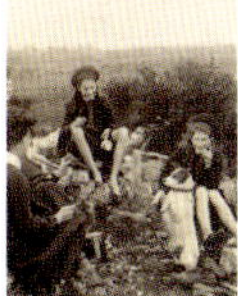

116–117, back cover. Onehunga, unknown photographer.
AUCKLAND LIBRARIES HERITAGE COLLECTIONS, 1342-ALBUM-244-80-2

This photograph of Agatha Mary Dobbie (1880–1980), far left, and unnamed girls, some of whom may be her sisters, and a fox terrier is captioned as being taken in Ōnehunga, and was possibly made around 1910. Agatha was the eldest of the seven children of Herbert and Charlotte Dobbie (1860–1952, née Gilfillan), one of whom died in childhood. Herbert Dobbie (1854–1940), best known in later life as a collector of ferns, published an important book of images of his specimens in 1921. The family lived in Whangārei and then in Market Road, Auckland, not far from where this image was taken. Agatha's younger sister Beatrix Dobie (1887–1944; she changed the family surname back to its original spelling) studied at the Slade School of Art in London and became a noted artist, perhaps best known as the illustrator of Herbert Guthrie-Smith's *Tutira*. Agatha (a music student in London when war broke out), Beatrix and their younger sister Ellen served as volunteer nurse aides with the British Red Cross in the First World War. This photograph, by an unknown photographer, appears in a Dobbie family photo album held in the Auckland Libraries Heritage collection.

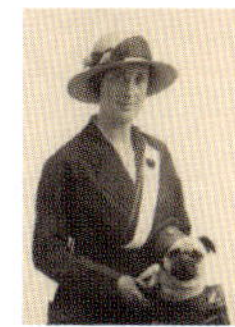

119. Frances Broad, 1914–1918, unknown photographer.
TE PAPA, O.048932. GIFT OF MARIANNE ABRAHAM IN MEMORY OF T. WYVILLE RUTHERFURD, MCKENZIE GIBSON, FRANCES AND DOROTHY BROAD, 2019

This photograph of Frances Broad (1886–1963) features her fundraising work during the First World War. She is accompanied by a dog dressed as a Belgian soldier. Frances was involved in fundraising and other wartime activities (such as first aid) on the West Coast of New Zealand.

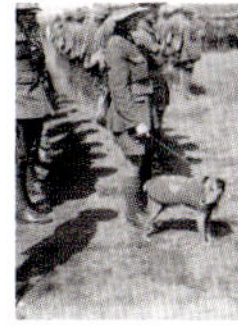

121. Paddy, the canine mascot of the Wellington Regiment, at a troop inspection in France (30 June 1918), unknown photographer.
ALEXANDER TURNBULL LIBRARY, 1/2-013312-G
See story, page 120.

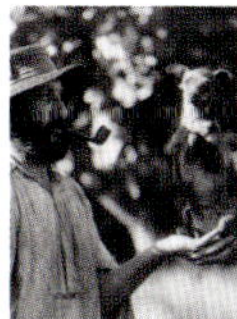

122. Mr Richards and dog, F G Gibbs.
NELSON PROVINCIAL MUSEUM, 321552

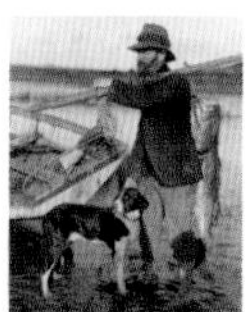

123. Fishing, Northland (*c.*1915), Northwood Brothers Studio.
ALEXANDER TURNBULL LIBRARY, 1/1-004934-G

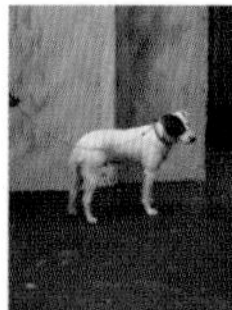

124. Dog, E Bradbury & Co.
WAIKATO MUSEUM TE WHARE TAONGA O WAIKATO, 1961/4/229

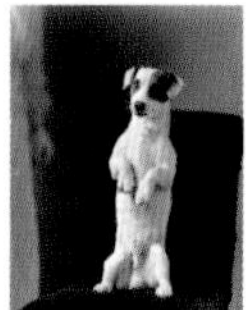

125. Harden, Tyree studio.
NELSON PROVINCIAL MUSEUM, 85318

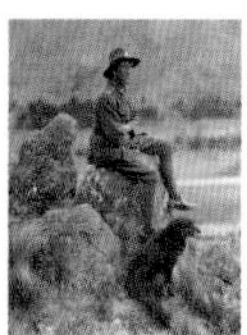

126–127. Cyril McCusker in the uniform of a mounted rifleman, with a dog, at Taylor Pass, Marlborough (*c.*1914), Arthur J McCusker.
ALEXANDER TURNBULL LIBRARY, 1/2-182028-G

This photograph of Cyril McCusker (1891–1964) in his Mounted Rifles uniform was taken at Taylor Pass in Marlborough in 1914 by his father, Blenheim photographer Arthur McCusker. Over a long career in Blenheim, McCusker won many photography medals for pastoral and agricultural photography. In 1933 his business was taken over by his son, Gordon. A large collection of Arthur and Gordon McCusker's negatives is held by the Marlborough Museum.

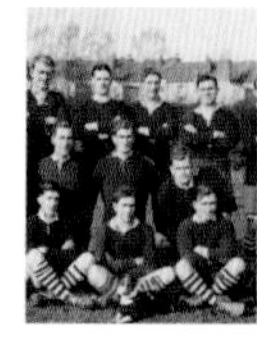

129. Floss, the New Zealand Army rugby mascot (1917), unknown photographer.
MANATŪ TAONGA, THE MINISTRY FOR CULTURE AND HERITAGE
See story, page 128.

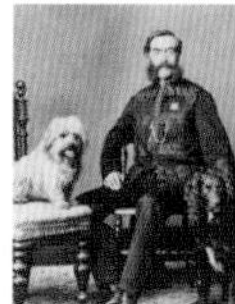

130. Major Nixon, Tyree studio.
NELSON PROVINCIAL MUSEUM, 68455

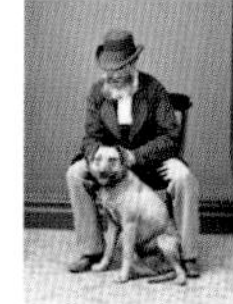

131. Unidentified man, seated, with his dog (1870–1890), William J Harding Studio.
ALEXANDER TURNBULL LIBRARY, 1/4-006459-G

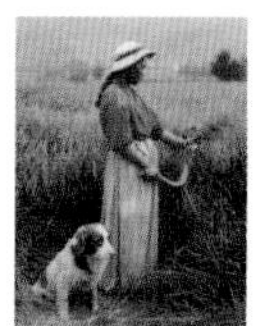

133. Unidentified woman harvesting grain (*c.*1910), Arthur James Northwood.
ALEXANDER TURNBULL LIBRARY, 1/1-010884-G
See story, page 132.

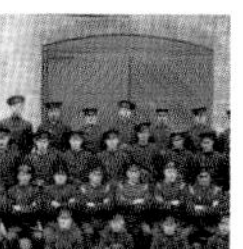

134–135. Fire Brigade, Schmidt studios.
AUCKLAND LIBRARIES HERITAGE COLLECTIONS, 31-WP947

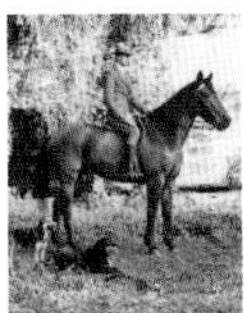

136–137. Hayter, Ellis Dudgeon.
NELSON PROVINCIAL MUSEUM, 187062

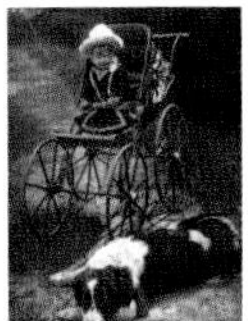

138. Oswald Binns (*c.*1891), Charles E Binns.
AUCKLAND LIBRARIES HERITAGE COLLECTIONS, 80-BIN92

Frederick Charles Binns (1843–1915), a civil engineer, established a photographic partnership with James Wrigglesworth in 1874 in Wellington. Wrigglesworth & Binns later opened branches in Christchurch and Dunedin, and was one of New Zealand's best-known photographic studios.

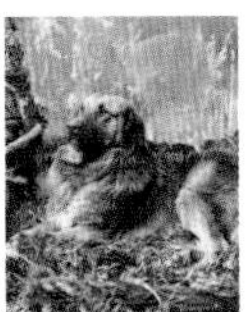

139. Gledhill's dogs, Collingwood, Tyree studio.
NELSON PROVINCIAL MUSEUM, 38911

This fine dog and its puppy possibly belonged to Collingwood publican William Gledhill (1853–1920).

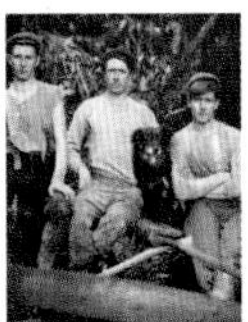

140–141. Bushmen and dog (*c.*1910), G E Archer.
MANAWATŪ HERITAGE, 2008N_BF7_WOR_1409

Rangitāne, mana whenua, first settled in the Manawatū region four hundred years ago. In 1871, inside Papaiōea, a 400-hectare natural clearing in the bush that cloaked the plains around what is now Palmerston North, a small settlement acquired a new name, a store and new settlers. As the little town grew, so bushmen steadily cleared the plains around it. Sawmilling was one of the town's earliest and most significant industries, and several mills operated on its periphery. In a story common to so much of New Zealand, as the demand for farmland grew, so the native trees fell. The eastern Manawatū plains are now almost devoid of native forest.

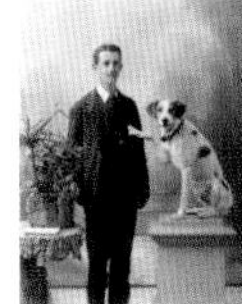

142. Mr Naylor and dog, Tyree studio.
NELSON PROVINCIAL MUSEUM, 38407

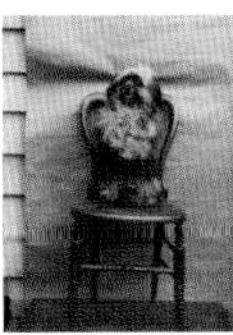

143. Dog posed on chair, Hardy Kitching.
NELSON PROVINCIAL MUSEUM, 317411

References and further reading

Books and articles

Dawber, Carol and Cheryl Win, *Ferntown to Farewell Spit*, River Press, 2003

Diamond, Paul, *Makereti: taking Māori to the world*, Random House New Zealand, 2007

Fitzgerald, Michael and Claire Regnault, *Berry Boys: Portraits of First World War soldiers and families*, Te Papa Press, 2014

McCarthy, Kerry, 'An Antarctic Love Story', *Antarctic* 29, no. 4, issue 218 (2011)

McCredie, Athol, *New Zealand Photography Collected*, Te Papa Press, 2015

Swarbrick, Nancy, *Creature Comforts: New Zealanders and their pets, an illustrated history*, Otago University Press, 2013

Sullivan, John, 'A Fijian in Bulls', Turnbull Library Record, Volume 43, 1 January 2010

Sullivan, John, 'Northwood country', *NZ Listener*, 26 October 1985

Tennant, Margaret, Geoff Watson and Kerry Taylor (eds), *City at the Centre: A history of Palmerston North*, Massey University Press, 2020

Walsh, Frances, *Endless Sea*, Massey University Press, 2020

Websites

'Dobbie, Herbert Boucher', https://teara.govt.nz/en/biographies/3d9/dobbie-herbert-boucher

'Dr Grace Russell and the Dobie sisters', http://heritageetal.blogspot.com/2017/11/dr-grace-russell-and-dobie-sisters.html

'Floss, the New Zealand Army rugby mascot', https://nzhistory.govt.nz/media/photo/floss-the-nz-army-rugby-team-mascot

'James Dennistoun: A life of adventure', https://www.canterburymuseum.com/discover/stories/james-dennistoun-a-life-of-adventure/

'Military mascots', https://nzhistory.govt.nz/war/mascots

'Muir and Moodie', https://canterburyphotography.blogspot.com/2009/03/muir-and-moodie-dunedin.html

'Osman, Scott's best sledge dog', https://www.canterburymuseum.com/discover/blog-posts/osman-scotts-best-sledge-dog/

'Terror in Timaru', https://www.canterburymuseum.com/discover/stories/terror-in-timaru/

'The dogs of war', https://www.stuff.co.nz/world/europe/63856860/the-dogs-of-war

'Tyree images priceless window to Nelson's past', https://www.stuff.co.nz/nelson-mail/news/100461854/tyree-images-priceless-window-to-nelsons-past

'Western Golden Bay', https://teara.govt.nz/en/nelson-places/page-10

About the writer

Mike White, pictured here with Cooper, is one of New Zealand's best-known investigative journalists and is a lifelong dog lover. For many years an award-winning senior writer at *North & South*, he is now a senior writer at Stuff. His previous books are *How to Walk a Dog* (Allen & Unwin, 2019), about life in and around a dog park, and *Who Killed Scott Guy?* (Allen & Unwin, 2015).

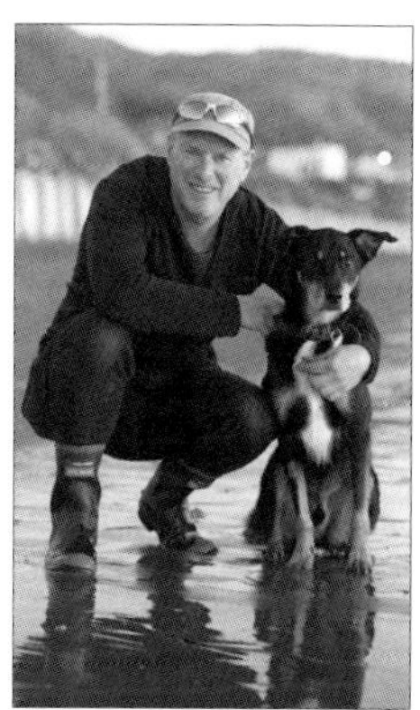

Photo: Nikki Macdonald

Acknowledgements

It seems that the love of dogs drives many people to go the extra helpful mile, and such has been the case with this book.

Te Papa Press is grateful to one of its authors, William Cottrell, who sparked the idea for this book when he started sending us amusing historic photographs of dogs from the Tyree Collection of the Nelson Provincial Museum.

Many museum curators have been of immense assistance, and our huge thanks go to: Jenni Chrisstoffels at the Alexander Turnbull Library, Te Puna Mātauranga o Aotearoa National Library of New Zealand; Lesley Courtney and Jaime Ridge at Palmerston North City Library; Keith Giles at Auckland Libraries Ngā Whare Mātauranga o Tāmaki Makaurau; Jill Haley at Canterbury Museum; Darryl Gallagher at Nelson Provincial Museum Pupuri Taonga o Te Tai Ao; Kimberley Stephenson at Southland Museum and Art Gallery Niho o te Taniwha; staff at MTG Hawke's Bay Te Ahuriri, Puke Ariki, Waikato Museum Te Whare Taonga o Waikato, and Toitū Otago Settlers Museum; and the curatorial staff at Te Papa Tongarewa, including photography curators Athol McCredie and Lissa Mitchell. Thanks also to Carol Dawber (River Press) and Penny Griffith, who helped with information about the Pākawau coal miners, and to June Grant (Te Arawa, Tūhourangi/Ngāti Wāhiao, Tūwharetoa) for providing Mākereti's diary entry.

In the book publishing world, we are grateful to: Emma Jameson for early image research; Kate Stone and Mike Wagg for proofreading; and Sarah Elworthy for design and the eye-catching cover.

Finally, we must thank Mike White, dog lover extraordinaire, who was as captivated by the images as we were, and whose delightful essay adds immeasurably to this book's charm.

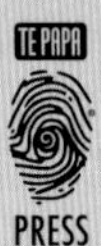

First published in New Zealand in 2022
by Te Papa Press, PO Box 467, Wellington,
New Zealand www.tepapapress.co.nz

© Museum of New Zealand
Te Papa Tongarewa

This book is copyright. Apart from any fair dealing for the purpose of private study, research, criticism, or review, as permitted under the Copyright Act, no part of this book may be reproduced by any process, stored in a retrieval system, or transmitted in any form, without the prior permission of the Museum of New Zealand Te Papa Tongarewa.

TE PAPA® is the trademark of the Museum of New Zealand Te Papa Tongarewa
Te Papa Press is an imprint of the Museum of New Zealand Te Papa Tongarewa

ISBN 978-1-99-115090-5

A catalogue record is available from the National Library of New Zealand

Design by Sarah Elworthy
Digital imaging by Jeremy Glyde
Printed in China by 1010 Printing Asia Ltd

Front cover image: Mr Canavan (1882), unknown photographer.

NELSON PROVINCIAL MUSEUM,
W E BROWN COLLECTION, 16583

Back cover image: Onehunga [Agatha Mary Dobbie and friends], unknown photographer.

AUCKLAND LIBRARIES HERITAGE
COLLECTIONS, 1342-ALBUM-244-80-2